THE USE OF THE DRAMA

THE USE OF
THE DRAMA

The substance of three lectures delivered at
Princeton University, U.S.A., upon the
Spencer Trask Foundation in 1944

Harley Granville-Barker

LONDON
SIDGWICK & JACKSON

FIRST PUBLISHED 1946
MADE AND PRINTED IN GREAT BRITAIN
BY T. AND A. CONSTABLE LTD.
EDINBURGH

CONTENTS

I

Upon the Arts in General, and Their Fortunes in England

The arts in general have during the past fifty years become more and more a public concern in England. It is as well they should be, since the sources of private munificence are being so rapidly dried up by the suction-pump of the tax collector. Slowly, very slowly, we are cultivating a public conscience in the matter of the arts. Throughout the centuries they have had with us—now one, now another—their ups and downs, and, on the whole perhaps, a rough time rather than a smooth. One among them might decay and perish altogether, as did the marvellous scriptorial art of the Anglo-Saxon monasteries. Another would vanish, to reappear in a different form. The Reformation seemingly sees the end of our church architecture; but a while later comes Wren, with him Gibbons and his school to replace the anonymous carvers and decorators, the craftsmen of the old faith. Fresh inspiration may come from abroad, for some arts are, of course, in their very nature more internationally viable than others. Architecture and the plastic arts cross frontiers with little difficulty; music finds somewhat more, drama much more.

Music and drama—with dancing, which links the two—are everywhere, probably, the most popular of the arts. You can write them with a capital A or a very small one; and *King Lear*, the latest farce, *Rosmersholm*, *Punch and Judy* are all drama. Even so a tune played by a street-corner ragamuffin on the penny whistle, and Beethoven's Mass in D are both music. Moreover, I believe Toscanini would tell us that in

7

conducting the Mass it is important to retain the spirit which animates a really good performance on the penny whistle.

MUSIC

Music in England has had its ups and downs, but it has at no time ceased to be. We must relapse far into savagery indeed for all the music in us to perish. In the sixteenth century and for far into the seventeenth we led Europe in the practice of the art. Some knowledge of it was a part of every gentleman's education, while, over the simple, sighs Bishop Corbet:

> When Tom came home from labour
> Or Ciss to milking rose
> Then merrily went their tabor
> And nimbly went their toes.

And even the Puritans, at the extreme of their sour tyranny, did not manage to suppress music as they did the drama.[1] One hears of the stern old Protector, wearied and embittered, sitting by the fire in the winter evenings at Whitehall while his daughters and their friends made music for him. And its traditional association with the Church was never quite broken. This had survived the great changes of the Reformation; and although the Saints did succeed in closing the cathedrals and reducing the choirs to silence for fifteen years, many of the trained musicians thrown out of employ at the beginning of that time were still there and ready to take up the work again at its end (if the subject interests you, read that scholarly and delightful book by Dr. Fellowes on English Cathedral Music).

There followed, however, a time during which—except that it was illuminated by the genius of Purcell—English music, sacred and secular both, and educated interest in it,

---

[1] But even the drama, it seems, was not so completely suppressed as we used to suppose.

noticeably weakened. But every art will have its fallow periods; and it is then that, the creative impulse slackening, such ties as those which bound music to the Church—the custom, in this case, of the daily choral services—will help to keep it alive. Now, however, was the time when the influence of the continental schools increased. Yet it is worth noting that Handel, the great foreign influence of the period, domiciled in England, was himself so influenced by English tradition and custom that he turned from his Italianate opera to develop oratorio—the glorified church anthem.

Of the very early history of music in America I must own, ashamedly, to being ignorant. In New England, at any rate, I fancy, it amounts to little more than psalm singing and hymn singing; although it is probable that memories of balladry unsanctioned by Puritan elders could be raked up. Some young man of the wilder sort aboard the *Mayflower* may have tucked a surreptitious flute into his baggage and slipped privately away sometimes to play it. Emigrants to the Appalachians a century later certainly brought songs along, for Cecil Sharp found them there two centuries later still. There was some acting of plays in Virginia and South Carolina in the early eighteenth century. Such ungodliness did not raise its head in Boston until long after that, and then it was sternly suppressed.

It is a sorry story, that of the slow lowering of musical standards in England. The art does not, as I said, fall into absolute desuetude. Its traditional duty to the Church is a firm anchor on the one side, while on the other popular song and dance retain something of the strength of all deeply rooted things (if they are to die they die hard); and they feed a persistent appetite though they may stimulate no taste. But native weakness, in an art so easy of import or export as music, opens the door *too* wide to the foreign product and its influence. The product itself is to be welcomed; only a per-

verted fool would wish to stop us listening to Bach and
Mozart and Beethoven because we have no equivalents of
our own. The influence is another matter. Accept it supinely
and our weakness grows weaker still. *Creative* emulation is
not to be forced; that we shall wisely admit. But *taste* can be
cultivated and *critical* standards kept high. Then, when the
time comes for fresh growth, the harvest will be richer. As
things unhappily were, when great days were dawning elsewhere, while with us musical knowledge was ceasing to be a
part of general education, critical standards in general went
down. There remained, as largely there still remains, appetite
without taste, while taste becomes the appurtenance of the
few. And then it is that the day of the 'amateur' dawns.

Upon more than one of our English arts the influence of
the amateur is marked; upon some for good, no doubt; but
for harm also. The term first comes to mean ' one who culti-
vates a special taste for an art'; and through much of the eighteenth and nineteenth centuries our best secular music, brought
from abroad, owes its chief support, doubtlessly, to cultured
groups of such amateurs. But by 1806, says the dictionary,
the word can stand for 'a dabbler' too. And from about then
it is that the study of music degenerates mainly into the teaching of multitudes of middle-class young ladies to play the
piano—prettily enough to put Papa to sleep after dinner. The
sterner tradition of church music survives (though it too goes
somewhat soft under this polite influence), and the plaintive
gaieties of the village fiddler can still occasionally be heard.
But by and large music in England has become a poor thing.

Within my own lifetime I have seen a change. The
connoisseur-amateurs have held their ground, and it is to their
critical standards that the best music we have must conform.
But the popular counterpart of this has lifted its aim and
measured up its quality most remarkably. This used mainly
to consist in entertainments known as 'Ballad Concerts',

which were made up of a piano solo, the singing, in succession, by soprano, contralto, tenor and baritone of drawing-room ballads, so-called ('The Better Land', 'In the Gloaming', 'The Lost Chord', 'The Garden of Sleep') pretty tunes competently sung; a violin solo for variety, possibly a vocal quartet to finish—and so quietly home. In the summer in London there might be 'Promenade Concerts'. I remember one series of them; it was at Covent Garden. We promenaded. There was an orchestra. The conductor wore white kid gloves. Two bevies of young ladies, the sopranos in blue, the contraltos in pink, sang what were called 'Vocal Valses', and sometimes we paused more respectfully while a solo-singer shot off a 'ballad' at us. It was not very thrilling, but the management thought the public would stand nothing better. The change that has taken place is a typically English change. The promenade concerts, so-called, continue and in theory you may 'promenade'. But you will be wise not to try. Your neighbours will not like it. The wide space is packed by men and women who—mostly at the end of a day's work, too!—are ready to stand for a couple of hours or so, all attention, listening to Bach, Beethoven and Brahms. I do not pretend that they are a highly critical crowd. There is no doubt more appetite than taste still in this love for music. But it is now a love for good music; that is the point.[1]

What has wrought the change? Education. This has not meant, of course, the direct instruction of these growing crowds in harmony and counterpoint, in either the theory or practice of music. The process is indirect and slow, spreading out, often imperceptibly, and filtering down through generations. But one can date, I think, this change from the maturing of the work done by the Royal College of Music,

---

[1] This refers to the days before—alas!—the Queen's Hall was 'blitzed'. And now the Albert Hall, less suited to promenading, but a far larger building, is packed for each concert.

the Academy, and other such institutions dotting the country with men like Parry and Mackenzie and Stanford at their head. They were not themselves, and they did not habitually mould, musicians of world-shaking renown; indeed, it would be perhaps the hardest part of a professor's task to persuade the overvaultingly ambitious young pianists or fiddlers that their likelier and not unworthy lot lay in a teachership at some school. Gustav Holst, to the day of his death, earned his bread as teacher at a ladies' college; and high and distinguished in consequence was the standard of its music. A century of liberal musical education, some discouragement of the mere dabblers (though let them dabble among themselves if they will), the teaching of the teachers, music in its simplicity accepted as a part of common education, the study of music for its own sake, more and more good music to be cheaply and easily heard—the taste for it spreads, and the national standard is slowly screwed up. It is a change and a process worth recording; and it is most pertinent to my proper subject of the use of the drama, to which this screw of good taste has hardly yet been applied.

PAINTING

The patron, besides the amateur, has had his influence on English art. The two are cater-cousins. With the Reformation the Church let painting slip (as it let the drama slip, too). Protestant England was no place for Crucifixions and Saints and Madonnas. But there had ever been the patron, the donor of the fresco, figuring modestly in the corner. He had only to be brought to the middle and enlarged, the saints removed, and there was the portrait. The king, in those days, was chief of donors, patron of patrons; and, the civil wars over, and he having gathered to him more influence than ever before, his court became the centre of art and culture, and the Renaissance bloomed belatedly in England.

But the great lords of the kingdom remained still, in effect, kings in their own courts too, each with his crowd of retainers; these were armed forces no longer—that was the effective change. The statesmanlike Tudors encouraged their replacing by musicians and men of letters, designers of pageants, companies of actors and the like. Better money so spent and energies so dissipated than in rebellion. Patronage of the arts became one of the hall-marks of the Quality, and the patronage of painting in particular soon began to flow through and beyond the hands of the indubitably great into those of anyone who could afford to have his own or his wife's portrait painted—in oils; that was the correct thing. And in the eighteenth century the art was given a cachet of official respectability, an extended appeal to the 'middling' classes, by the founding of the Royal Academy. The connoisseur-amateur had been earlier in the field; an aristocrat usually, witness the long picture galleries, and the portfolios of prints and drawings, now depleted, in the great libraries. The dabbler-amateur comes to his own too. With increase of leisure for the lady (compare the economy of the Verney household to life lived at Mansfield Park) water-colour drawing proves to be a most delightful medium to dabble in—not oils, they make the room smell. And one does need a change from that everlasting needlework. Dabbling has its further benefits. One way at least, it can be argued, of learning to appreciate an art is to practise it a little yourself. When picture exhibitions began, the dabblers passing by could tell a bit better for their dabbling what Constable and Wilson and Crome and the rest were up to. On the other hand was this drawback. Their taste was bound to conform somewhat to the measure of their own meek achievements, and they were the less likely to give an intelligent eye to the work of the man who lived for his work alone and in a world of it. So develops a characteristic feature of both English artistic achievement and English critical taste—for the two become, of course, reciprocal—and this is in a word Timidity, and it still impoverishes more of our arts than one. For with it goes the wish to please and be pleased, lack of interest in principles, readiness to compromise; and these, to certain hypercritical foreigners, are the defects of some of our otherwise admirable qualities.

Painting—not only in England—has become the art which it is easiest to patronize, given a respectable bank balance. You need know nothing of the art itself, nor even like the particular picture you buy, nor—if your house has a darkish corner or so—see much of it after you have bought it. You need not care for the art of painting at all; but pictures are creditable furnishings. If it is the work of a living artist in question, once you have handed him a cheque your liability is discharged. Thereafter the worst thing the picture can do to you is to go down in cash value, and reproach your judgment. But avoid the living artist, and go to a good dealer (who has made money at the game and has a reputation to lose), invest in the gilt-edged security of indisputable old masters, and there is no great danger of that. Buy a hundred such pictures and announce your intention of bequeathing them to a museum, and you earn the reputation of an enlightened patron of the arts.

Not that one should mock too heavily at museum or academy, at the great, gilt, entablatured 'Snooks Collection' over the entrance, or at that annual dinner party with stars and ribbons sported, and orations as banal—one exasperatedly exclaims —as the canvases outfacing the orators. For this is an impressive recognition of the importance of art as a token of true civilization, surely. Nobody need grudge Snooks his tribute; nor are the dinner-party speeches, by such standards, necessarily bad—nor even the pictures. It is only that, as we leave one of these incongruous banquets, our bellies filled with the east wind also, the uncomfortable question may possibly present itself: by how much has the actual art of painting, or its appreciation, been advanced? Painting in England has been slow to reach popularity. The Last Judgment on the church wall was not meant to give us pleasure. Even could the mayor and corporation of some British Borgo San Sepolcro have found the Piero so to glorify their council chamber with such a Resurrection they might reasonably have doubted whether, what with the cold and the damp and the climate in general, he could hope to make a good job of it. Thereafter painting and sculptures too lost hold on the people. 'Easel-painting' became the possession of the privileged few. Until but the other day, a young middle-class couple would no more think of hanging their sitting-room with drawings of their choice or asking a price at a picture show than of making an offer for the Venus of Milo. A 'work of art' was not for them.

But here too have been changes, educational in their kind. Much reduction in 'dabbling', I fancy. The young man of to-day who finds he has eyes in his head is likelier to learn to use them simply by *looking*—no more—at pictures of all sorts and kinds, academic and eccentric, until he comes to like this sort more than that, and a few of some sort well enough to find a continuing pleasure in them. How harmless a pleasure —and more than a pleasure! ('But, Mr Turner, I never see such colours in the sky.' 'Ah, madam', answered Turner, 'don't you wish you could?'. And with Turner and his fellows for interpreters, we have found that we can.) By one means and another the art of the painter is being given back to the people. Processed and vulgarized for the most part, nowadays, it may be objected. We are indeed assaulted daily on all sides by the crude colours and crashing type of the poster; worse, pandered to by the delicacies debased of the cheap magazine. And pictures for the most of the world are *the* Pictures. But into this mass of common stuff, the spirit of the artist can be said—though uncertainly—to be filtering. It is a strange civil war; between democracy with its demand for novelty and quantity and its high pay, and the artist with quality for his watchword.

LITERATURE

Literature, likewise, has freed itself from patronage. This 'patronage' has an ugly sound, I suppose, to American ears, and younger English ears may not much like it. But it should not convey mere obloquy. The practice—like the wearing of swords and the riding of horses—has had its use. In the sixteenth and seventeenth centuries an unpatronized poet—or one who at least had not the equivalent of some sinecure or small independence—would have been hard put to it to keep alive. Publishing was scarcely yet a matter of solid commerce. The famous five pounds given to Milton for the first edition of *Paradise Lost* was possibly just about what it was then worth. Less than a century earlier *Venus and Adonis* and *Lucrece*, with as much else as he could have written to fill up a volume, would certainly not have brought their author so much. (Drama was another matter; there was money in the drama. Henslowe would pay six pounds for a new play.) If the rumour were true, then, that the young Lord Southampton asked him to accept a hundred pounds 'towards the making of a purchase he had a mind to' and as a tribute to his promise as a poet, surely the transaction was creditable to both sides. Shakespeare gave what he had to give, the fruits of his genius, and Southampton (who evidently either knew good poetry when he heard it, or was willing to be instructed) dispensed a little of his more material wealth, which, as a nobleman of those days, he would feel he held in free trust for his dependents. In return for such bounty public thanks were expected. They would be evidence that the patron was doing his duty. They came commonly in the form of a dedication of the printed poem. Shakespeare's to Southampton is elaborate and formal, as richly coloured, as ornate as were the clothes men wore in those days. But there is nothing more falsely servile in it than in the subscription to a letter—out of date nowadays truly—as from a man's 'most obedient servant'. You are not the fellow's servant, you don't mean to be obedient to him, you don't mean him to think so, and he doesn't think so. It is merely a form of manners.

But matters in this kind soon changed; the manners more slowly. Dryden, forced to do so, could, directly or indirectly, make money by his writing; Pope made quite a lot; Johnson supported himself. Gradually the patron became a superfluous ornament upon the edifice of literature (see Johnson's famous letter to Lord Chesterfield; but Chesterfield came not so badly out of the bear's hug). He had outlasted his use; literature was becoming 'popular', and the public was to be its only patron. But consider for a moment what the exact nature of the change has been. If that century-past dedication, 'To his grace the Duke ——' or 'To the most noble the Marquis ——' was foolishly flattering, at least the flattery usually ended there. It did not corrupt the contents of the book, were the author a man of any worth at all. To-day the popular author dedicates his book implicitly to the half-million readers he hopes will buy it; and, that they may, it is too apt to be riddled with flattery of their ignorances and prejudices— which combine to make what we call public taste. Is there such a thing, one asks? We have at any rate not yet demonstrated that appeal to the many brings a better quality of literature than did dependence on the few.

It is, indeed, astonishing that the standard of accomplishment in English writing keeps to-day even as high as it does, so small is the inducement in credit or money to a man going into the literary market to write as well as he can; while the depths of 'as badly as he dare' seem hard to plumb. We have had in England, and still hope for, writers of genius in both poetry and prose. But too often, in the past, it was their sheer genius which distinguished them, their imaginative and emotional power, while the literary accomplishment would not be very high. No matter, we said, the genius was the essential thing. But then, alas, come the writers who have *not* genius, and they will always be in the majority. The very greatest capacity for taking pains (the next best thing) is doubtless a poor substitute for true genius. But it is better than nothing, and might well be encouraged somewhat more warmly than at present it is, while sheer lack of literary self-respect might even better be more harshly condemned. Compare English reviewing to French. The self-respecting French critic will, as a matter of course, comment on the form of a book, on the style of its writing, and—its contents beside—on its workmanship and literary value. His English counterpart may hardly be troubled by gross errors of syntax and grammar. But each, supposedly, will be considering his readers; and while every educated Frenchman is expert in French, few Englishmen know English or ever will; so how should they care whether it be well written or no? Something called 'Basic English' has been sprung on us lately. It is a remarkable invention, an unexpected product of a school of subtle criticism, and—so I gather from some of its supporters—may help to implement our post-war trade the world over. Naturally, I am all for that. Anybody will be able to learn it, from the benighted heathen (if there are any left) to the very members of His Majesty's Government; and it will be teachable, apparently, in ten minutes or so. Very practical and useful doubtless! But the writers one delights in will, I fancy, stay pledged to the practice—the very difficult practice—of this complex, anomalous, ever-developing language that we have inherited, cultivating the great estate of it and weeding out the ill growths. For its good writing, we need besides a school of stern critics, who will themselves be read. As to its speaking, something might be done by cultivating the art of the drama, in which the art of speaking is included. So to that subject I come   at last!

THE DRAMA AND ITS EDUCATIONAL USE

Drama is—it can, at least, be kept—the very simplest of the arts. 'Three boards and a passion' are, it has been said, all that is needed for the performance of a play. No mastering of instruments is demanded. The painter must have his brush and his canvas, the sculptor his chisel; the writer of music demands its playing by other musicians of long training and much skill. But for the dramatist a few sheets of paper suffice; and the actor, serving him, is his own instrument. The medium, moreover, is one in which we all work unconsciously from the hour of our birth; some extra training in it cannot, presumably, be a very great matter. But there is a catch here—as, when it comes to dealing with the incalculable arts, there is ever apt to be. The human personality is doubtless, in terms of *nature*, the easiest of instruments to play upon, but, in terms of art, it can be the most difficult. For consider: with piano, fiddle or flute there are defined, mechanical limits to what can be done even by the best of performers; they are the limits of the instrument itself. With the human personality there are none, none at least that can be so mechanically defined. One may put this to something of a test by trying to transpose into the exacter medium of words the many successive delicacies and subtleties of (say) the performance by Gieseking of a Debussy nocturne or of a Bach suite by Wanda Landowska. It can—at inordinate length and quite inadequately—just about be done. Now try to do the same by one of Duse's greater stretches of acting (if that is

not unhappily too dim a memory now) or by the more complex interchanges of a scene from *The Three Sisters* played
by Stanislawsky's Moscow company; you will find it cannot
be. The drama is in origin the simplest of the arts; it can be
developed into the most complex.

We have hardly yet freed ourselves in England from our
crooked Puritan attitude toward the drama, and oddly
equivocal shadows of it can naturally still be found falling in
America too. As to that, I used to wonder whether a fifty
year earlier emigration might not perhaps have taken the
Elizabethan theatre with it. But this, of course, is ignorant
miscalculation. The Puritans were already digging in while
Shakespeare lived and worked and mocked at them. 'Marry,
Sir,' said Maria of Malvolio, 'he is sometimes a kind of
Puritan.' And dare-devil Sir Andrew shrills joyously, 'O, if
I thought that, I'd beat him like a dog.' Even then they
lacked not the will to suppress the theatre; and later there in
England they found—as here to New England they carried—
the power. This, both there and here, they have long lost.
Yet Puritan influence in England is by no means dead; and
there are those of us who have no wish to see the humaner
aspects of it die (its influence *within* the theatre might come
as an occasional boon). But we started the pendulum swinging.
We ostracized the drama and treated the theatre which har-
bours it as an antechamber to Hell. That lent it a specious
attractiveness, and it gained the unwholesome flavour of for-
bidden fruit. To-day it is a spoilt child among the arts, pam-
pered and flattered, extravagant and presumptuous, with its
true good neglected; and, while we may be caught by its
glamour, we do not take it seriously. Things will never be
wholly well with it—let us postulate this—until we have learnt
to approach it simply, and without any self-consciousness at all.

Only recently has drama been allowed its educational
status again. I say 'again'; it is often forgotten how much of

such service it was put to in the not so remote past. Schoolboys were always acting plays, the universities too. At Trinity, Cambridge, the undergraduates were obliged by statute to present five a year in the great hall. The Puritans stopped that. And when, after banishment, drama did return to schools and universities it came creeping back in disguise, so to say. It did not for long venture off the printed page: anything like acting would never have done. The study would be labelled 'Greek Tragedy', or 'The Rise of Blank Verse', or 'The Return of the Rhymed Couplet'—anything to conceal the shameful fact that the thing being studied was really a play. And when at last it came to modern drama, the sort of play actually being acted in theatres at that very moment, and there to be seen . . .! I am told that when George Pierce Baker (whose services to the American drama can never be too highly acclaimed) first imparted to his once revolutionary-minded President his intention of giving a course in it—on the printed page only—Eliot misgivingly shook his head. But he (Eliot) may have had a truly foreseeing mind; since once the pendulum did gather impetus for a full swing back it was to swing rapidly and far. Soon Baker was in occupation of the famous 'Forty Seven Workshop' where play-writing and play-acting were practical studies; and, within a few years more, half the colleges and universities of America were following the example set, and the art of the drama was taking an often formidable place in the curriculum.

A good thing, undoubtedly, by comparison with the former myopic neglect. But I have met crabbed and unimaginative authorities who, noting the result of letting it compete for their students' attention with less glamorous options, have found it too much of a good thing altogether. So its champions may be wise, I think, to look very carefully also into whatever case can be made *against* it, to consider its possibly disruptive effect upon some little world of learning.

For drama has become to-day a very different and a far more elaborate affair than it was wont to be when it provided those old rhetorical exercises. Yet its chief claim to educational use will still be as a means to cultivating the satisfying art of self-expression.

SELF-EXPRESSION

This is a faculty with which, in our democratic countries, everybody looks to be endowed, and to find indulged. The right to express himself is one of the citizen's inalienable rights, freedom to express himself a freedom going with the rest. From the cradle onwards, every little democrat, kicking his nurse in the chin, and flinging his rattle to the floor, is but exercising his right to self-expression. And, since he will continue to do so in varying fashion throughout his riper years, on the rostrum or in the pulpit, on the floor of a convention or merely as one of a football crowd, there is something to be said for a little early training in the *art* of it, if only as a means to the mitigating of its cruder impulses.

Education to-day takes a far wider sweep that it did. But the present generous addition of 'isms' and 'ologies' only resulted for a while in the omitting of certain much simpler studies; and the culture of our common speech—our chief means to self-expression—was one of them. There were contributory causes, the chief, possibly, the extraordinary multiplication of books and newspapers, and the brighter lighting of winter evenings that let the whole family sit reading—or rather skimming—them. Human communication itself really seemed on the way to being mechanized (even as they say that, in another degree, the business-man, used to dictation and the typewriter, all but forgets how to *write* a letter!).

It is worth remembering that in the last great moulding of the English language it was the spoken rather than the written word which counted. If we grant Shakespeare and the Bible pre-eminence here, that Shakespeare wrote to be spoken does not ask argument. But the Bible also was 'appointed to be read [aloud] in churches', and here, for a century or more, was the simple man's chief approach to it. How much of the rhythm and melody which go to the making of the English language to-day, of its beauty and power, do we not owe to those translators having had the sound in their minds as well as the sense—even to the prejudice of the sense sometimes, later scholars have discovered. And how unwilling we have been to exchange the magic of the well-known words for mere accuracy! 'The morning stars sang together, and all the sons of God shouted for joy.' That may not be the precise meaning of the Hebrew, but in English the very sound of it lifts us off our feet.

This question of the effective use and sensitive appreciation of our language has a wide importance. It is said to be the most universally spoken in the world. Very certainly in no other language to-day have words of such consequence to the entire world to be spoken, have so many of the 'dooms' of mankind—to use that powerful old phrase—to be delivered. It is of some concern, then, to us British and Americans that the thousands of men and women representing us the world over and speaking daily in our name should be able to wield this weapon of language well, persuasively and accurately—I emphasize 'accurately' because when, as occasionally happens through its careless and faulty use, misunderstandings arise, something more than æsthetics will be involved.

Good speech is, of course, a matter for primary education. Its teaching begins in the nursery, though the need seldom ceases there. But the adolescent will seldom submit to continued drilling in an accomplishment that he feels sure he has mastered already. So, by university age, art has to be called in as a more amenable aid, and here it is, this art of self-expression, which is one of the elements of the art of the drama. Yet self-expression, as the drama involves it, asks more than skill in set speech by far.

THE RECEPTIVE SIDE; AND 'HAPPY WAYS OF DOING THINGS' IN POLITICS OR INDUSTRY

It has a receptive side. The actor must study, not only how to speak but how to listen. He is, while his part in a play provides for his listening, practising what may rather be called the art of self-*suppression*. He must encourage the speaker, draw out the best of him. It is an art which in daily life few of us very assiduously practise, our minds being usually more intent upon what we ourselves mean to say next (and so may the inferior actor's be). But that rarity, the good listener, is not the man who has nothing to say. It is, I suppose—this art of listening, practised in daily life, of appreciative listening—in the last analysis the art of good manners; and here, certainly, is an art which it will be well should pervade our education from kindergarten to university—and beyond. I will venture on an aphorism: good manners are the necessary solvent of a democratic civilization. That is not such a banality as it may sound to this present gathering of well-brought-up, nicely behaved people. I do not mean the conventional 'manners' which can be learnt as is the dancing of a ballet—though I have nothing against these if they are appropriate and pretty. I mean rather the good manners which Emerson interprets as 'happy ways of doing things', ways which help to ease the inevitable friction of a wearying day's work. In close-knit, comradely groups, in our colleges, regiments, and clubs we Americans and English at least already have, it may be said, these 'happy ways' as well developed as need be. But what I point out is that as the world is now going we shall need to widen the scope of them, and in an ever-increasing measure. Political democracy (acquired in America at a stroke, in England slowly and incongruously attained) denies class rule, the rule of the elect or expert of any kind. Now, on a small scale, in a simply organized world, the unalloyed democratic practice resulting has doubtless worked out well enough. But on a large scale, in a complex world, with experts continually called for, and men arising who make politics a whole-time job, it has for long been becoming in practice government by cliques and groups. And, in most countries calling themselves democratic, a new, motley, and traditionless 'governing class' has been forming which is a not too pleasing contrast to the old. But the attraction towards joining it—called 'going into public life'—will always prove to certain sorts of men irresistible. And, joining it, a man—so it practically follows—must familiarize himself with this way of life and learn how to get on well with his colleagues whoever they may be. And in that he will find this art of appreciative listening a very useful art indeed.

And another influence has recently been brought to bear by the development of 'industrial democracy'. This works as yet only partially and sporadically; we still tend to think in the old terms of masters and men, or—such words having become inadmissible—of employers and employees, ranged on two sides, the one against the other. But industrial democracy, as a system, is meant to obliterate this stark division. Authentic differences within the body politic no system of itself can cure; and this new one may even seem to increase these, since it certainly sets them free to ferment (but sitting on the safety-valve was ever a dangerous game). For it will involve the continual calling together of all sort of men, workers by hand and brain, from the expert and the organizer to Mr. Wallace's favourite 'common man', to discuss and decide, day in and day out, not the sort of questions which mainly go to make the programmes for our present political junketings, but those which directly affect our daily lives, questions touching pocket and stomach, and likely, therefore, to be debated closely, strenuously, and bitterly. It will, of course, be the realities involved which must finally count; and if an earthquake is imminent, no pills of politeness will cure it. But otherwise it is just under such circumstances that these 'happy ways of doing things' should prove most needful; as between men who are *not* comrades and colleagues, who have *not* similar traditions and the same sense of values, who may begin by personally disliking each other extremely— and, for that matter, so end.

We cannot be said, I know, to have launched into this 'industrial' extension of our 'political' democracy, with all its co-operative implications, very wholeheartedly. Yet, despite disagreements, there seems to be a general and a growing sense that we are committed to something of the sort. It looks indeed as if democracy might finally prove not to be workable at all in this modern world unless it can be worked *as a whole* politically, industrially, and even socially; though the full— and to some the fearful—implications of this last aspect of it are only slowly and sporadically ripening.[1] Moreover—without having over-exhaustively tested it ourselves—we confidently recommend this combination of political and industrial

---

[1] In England, of course, we are at present in a state, not only of economic transition but of more than usually pronounced social transition too. There are those who will tell you that to-day the social realities are nearly all democratic, that only a very few of the old aristocratic appearances remain. Let them add, then, that, but for food and drink, more people in this world live by appearances than realities; and add, further, that in England not only those in the upper strata of society ('stratified' is a better term than 'aristocratic': there has never been a permanently privileged aristocracy in England) will have preferred the old state of things, but many in the lower strata too. There was much to be said, and from divers points of view, in favour of the old order during any of its periods of stability—they never lasted long. Every man had his place in it under custom or the law. He had his work to do, and his relation to his neighbours was clearly defined and theirs toward him.

democracy to the rest of a distracted world as a certain cure for its ills. Then, if this is to be our civilization, clearly we must be strong in it, not weak, and only the stronger if we are to abjure the use of force as a final determinant. We cannot envisage our factories or countries, or a war-forbidden world itself, being run by committees composed of a few smart intriguers and polemical bullies, with a number of yes-men to make up the count. Such agreement as they reached would not be worth having. It could not last long; and while it did it would be no better than a focus of moral stagnation. Differences of opinion honestly disputed and, after, every consideration to be given to the out-voted minority—this is democracy's golden rule. We need to disagree. From what but disagreement can progress spring, and respect for each other? Let us only be all-but certain that our disagreements cannot end in fighting (and I say 'all-but', since absolute certainty is only a premium upon provocation) and we can profitably cultivate them.

Yet, reduced to a mere formula, these 'happy ways'—the very happiest—will prove barren. To be fruitful they must be dynamic, and a training in them can well make some use of this art of combining appreciation of the other man's point of view with clear assertion of one's own (self-suppression with self-expression), which is one of the constituents of that trivial and mighty art of the drama.

Do I so seriously associate the arts with these questions of high statecraft? Most seriously. On the one hand, education in the arts—or, let us rather say, the inclusion of the arts in education—can be a positive help toward making a man a statesman, and a better President of the United States or Prime Minister of England than he might otherwise be. The influence of the arts in education is, of course, chiefly indirect. But it is pervasive. It gives a man poise, and a point of view, sets up for him a standard of quality. It helps refine his faculties, mature his perceptions, it gives balance to his judgment. If, therefore, some understanding of Bach and Michelangelo and Shakespeare and of what they have done for the world does not make a man both express himself better, and find more in himself to express, as President or Premier, or doctor or lawyer or banker—why, so much the worse, not for the arts that these men's genius glorified, but for Law and Medicine and Banking themselves, for Washington and Downing Street, and for us all. If education has no place in it for art, it must mean that the very quality of our civilization is on the decline.

On the other hand, from the 'appreciative' standpoint;—incidentally we must not be taken in by fine phrases. Statecraft is no mystery; simply a matter of honesty, good sense, tradition, training, and experience. There is much to be said against the present condemning of our public men to do most of their work in public, photographed and radioed and reported minute by minute. It can hardly induce cool reasoning and reflection, must tend to make them both self-conscious and tiresomely oracular. Any influence of art it may show is likely to be that of very bad art. But at least it may dissipate the pretentiously official air which too often enwraps mere incompetence. In any country only a selected few can be called on to *practise* statecraft. It is the more important that the rest of us should properly appreciate its workings, be armed against its impositions, alive to the reality of the things done daily in the name of us all, lest later we emerge from our complaisant confusions to find we have been befooled and betrayed by that—as it will turn out—*ill*-selected few. But, again, a little education in the arts, with its sharpening of the senses, its lifting of standards, and cultivation of good judgment, might help us to distinguish in time between the sterling statecraft and the pinchbeck; between folly, whether dressed in finery or homespun, and the thing that

—though unpopular—was at the moment as near to wisdom as it is given to fallible man to attain. For art is the microcosm of life, and the ultimate standards in each are the same.

Now, of all the arts, that which has the first educational claim on us, and the one most easily fulfilled, is this simple and complex, trivial and mighty, art of the drama. A man may have no taste for music and painting, and never master much more than their alphabets. But the drama is—so to say—Everyman's art; it is the direct and living reflection of life itself, and few of us can be quite insusceptible to it.

II

Drama in Education

THE ELEMENTS OF THE ART, AND THE ART ITSELF

We are discussing the educational uses of the art of the drama. There is in this connection the use to be made of the elements of the art, also of the developed art itself. Some of its simplest elements—concise writing, eloquently clear speaking, appreciative listening—find their place in early education, and should not lose it later; for they are seldom so fully mastered that they can safely be forgotten. With the mastery of the art for a life's occupation, whether in play acting, directing or writing, I do not propose to deal. To cover that ground fully nowadays one should include directions toward the Eldorado of the Cinema (odd that California should have seen two gold rushes within the course of a century!) and of that I know nothing. Moreover, the direct study of the art itself has come to be pretty well and very variously provided for. One's passport to-day into the service of the drama may be either a thesis for a doctorate, or a prize at a beauty show. I am concerned with the art's generally educational uses, which do not demand of the student the artist's self-surrender and devotion, but allow for the detached attitude of the scholar, simply adding one more item to the sum of his knowledge. I do not think, therefore, that this purely educational study would find a satisfactory home in any fully developed 'school of drama', where such devotion would be the rule and little be talked or thought or dreamed of but the theatre.

Yet the art must be studied, however detachedly, in its

own terms. It may be doubted whether any art—though the principles of them all are probably the same—can be fully translated into terms other than its own, whether, for instance, we can expound a piece of music or a picture in words and hope to convey its essential quality. That will lie in the colour and pattern or in the sound, and must be sought there. Equally, drama must be studied, as far as possible, in terms of drama (and as little as possible, you may pertinently interpose, by means of disquisitions upon it, such as this). But words are at least a part of its proper medium, and commonly the most important part. Moreover, drama is peculiarly suited to class study. And the methods of a class of senior students (a seminar, as it is sometimes called) can well be made to resemble up to a point the rehearsals by a company of actors for a performance of a play—which will be its true completion.

The patent difference, as I see it, between the two approaches should be that a class of students will stop definitely short of putting the play into action, whereas a company of actors is from the beginning headed toward this. Every play involves action and even conflict, though it need not be physical action or physical conflict—which will, indeed, not take us dramatically very far. A knocks down B, who is rescued by C, who then knocks down A; there are not many possible variations upon that. *Punch and Judy* is the thoroughgoing play of action. The violent dramas in which our ancestors delighted usually contained a fight or two. The need for action of some sort is asserted in the convention of the French *scène-à-faire*. But it may be moral action; moral conflict, as in Ibsen's *Rosmersholm*; it may concern a man's inward struggles, as in *Hamlet*; or, as in Greek tragedy, his strife with fate and the gods. And generally speaking, the more mature a play's art the less is its action likely to depend upon either physical conflict or accident. Consider Shakespeare's artistic development, physical action being one of the dominant conventions of his theatre, and he not the man capriciously to discard convention. Note, then, how in such a mature tragedy as *Macbeth*, he relegates its physical action to second place. Of murders and killings there are, I think, no less than ten; yet all but two are contrived 'off stage'. Nor is it by the bodily death of its two splendid sinners that justice is done, but in the slower and more torturing death of their souls. *Macbeth* is above all a metaphysical—and in that an essentially poetic—tragedy.

Plainly, the least likely sort of play for our study will be one in which physical action has the larger share, in which, there-fore, we must come to it the sooner. In such plays the trained actor has the advantage of the student. With him understand-ing and expression tend to go hand in hand. Indeed, with the *over*-practised actor, expression may sometimes outrun under-standing, and effects be produced of no explicable cause. Yet we must not be positive in such cases that there *is* no cause. An actor of Hamlet, when he sees his father's ghost, may be able to express by intuition a process of feeling which he cannot at the moment—if ever he could—explain. The artist knows royal roads. But they are not for the student—nor too exclusively for the artist—to rely on. The student has to learn both to understand, and to make his understanding clear, first to himself, and then, in this class work, to his fellow-students.

THE SORT OF PLAY TO STUDY

The likeliest sort of play for study will be the metaphysic-ally conditioned play, since at that the actor will be kept studying the longest, and the student therefore can for longest keep closest to the actor's method, studying, as we said, the art in its own terms. Nor does the division between the two come merely because at some time the actor must 'go into action', so to say, while the student is to stop short of the captivating process of presenting the play upon a stage. It will come when, earlier than this, the actors begin to change their own student-critical attitude, and surrender themselves wholly to the play and their parts in it. Now this the student need never do. He can, and should, remain detached. And the process of his study may be described as an attempted resolving of the play into its constituents, a painstaking reversal of the possibly inspired process by which the dramatist has put it together and given it life. The *ultimate* secret of the life in it may not thereby be disclosed. We need to gather humbly round any dissecting table, and always (incidentally) to resist the temptation, which besets the uncreative mind, to pick a work of art to pieces and put it together again, sometimes reshaped to please ourselves. The student may indeed with advantage temporarily borrow the actor's intuition—travel a short way along the royal road— since we want him to gain not a mere bookish understanding, but a lively appreciation of the play, to come near, at least, to losing himself for the time. The pedagogue has only to take care that he should not be lured too far, and away from all solider studies, by this siren among the arts. Here we have, then, what should be, I contend, the decisive difference between the actor's way of work and the student's. The actor first learns all he can *about* the play, then goes ahead to lose himself *in* it, to identify himself with his particular part in it. The student and his fellows never so lose themselves; they too will learn all they can about the play, but rather so as to equip themselves as its ideal audience, sensitive and appreciative yet comprehensively knowledgeable and critical.

I do not suggest rules for the running of such a class; they should vary with the play to be studied and the quality of the students. I envisage some professor or instructor guiding the proceedings. I do not liken him to a director (or producer) of the play, there being no production in prospect; and he will be, from the beginning, one may suppose, readier to elicit his students' opinions upon the work in hand than to impress them with his own. Or am I wrong in that?

TYRANNY OR CO-OPERATION?

The directing of plays has become, within the last few generations, something of a tyranny, and I speak as one who has sinned. There were excuses. Staging swung between wooden convention and slapdash carelessness, or a leading actor went his own way and led the rest where he would. The director, with an eye to the play as a whole, did better than this. But the dictatorial process is hardly educational. Our class, on education bent, will have no use for it; and the chairman—professor, instructor, director, whatever he be—will be expected to hold his reins with a very light hand.

For while we shall be wise to borrow as many of the actor's methods as can be made to suit us, the best play director is he who ostensibly does least, not most. Actors are not puppets; and since, for the performance certainly, they will have to be let go from leading-strings, the less they are tied by them at all the better. There is a story of Ellen Terry, one of the few actresses of her time in whom some flame of genius burned. She once found herself in the hands of a notoriously authoritative stage-director. He gave her minute directions for the acting of a short stretch of a certain scene. She docilely repeated them. 'Yes, Mr. Blank, I think I understand. I am to move here and touch this, and to look there. And I do that and that and that. And then', she added sweetly, 'I must do that little bit extra, mustn't I, for which you want me to play the part?'

With every art, of course, it is that 'little bit extra' which finally counts, and what the artist inexplicably *is* besides what he does. But with the actor this is most paradoxically so. His art, fully developed, is a veritable invitation to egoism, but at the price of discarding the ego altogether. He is asked, not so much to assume another personality, as to interpret a character of an author's creating in terms of his own. To do this he may need to draw upon all his personal resources, appreciative, emotional, plastic, and to magnify himself to the utmost. Yet the character remains the author's, and while he is interpreting it we should forget about the actor. It is a hall-mark of the quality of his performance that we do. There is a delicate but distinct difference between the art of an actor giving himself to his part and that of one who exploits himself *in* his part, and the sensitive critic of acting will quickly discern it.

Acting is an art of collaboration—even as life is. The dramatist gives the actors a scheme of characters, more or less detailed. To it the actors bring themselves, realizing it, physically, psychologically, emotionally, and setting it in action. The content and importance of the contribution each party makes will vary much—as in life. Is not all collaboration hard to evaluate? A deed of partnership dealing with every detail must still leave the will to make it work undefined; and the partnership between dramatist and actor approaches the mystic. The actor may bring much to little, as, seemingly, did Joseph Jefferson to *Rip van Winkle* or Henry Irving to a poor play named *The Bells*. He may bring little to much (the disappointed dramatist's complaint of his actors), or much to more, and to that much a kindling variety. There have been a thousand Hamlets bad and good; one Hamlet remains.

Actors collaborate with each other also; and here, too, is a part of their practice from which students can very profitably borrow. And it brings us to considering again that 'happy way of doing things', which may help us a little more in general, perhaps, to follow the co-operative path of our democracies in the making. The scope and subtlety of the collaboration between the actors in a first-rate performance of a first-rate play is seldom fully appreciated, even seldomer put on record, if only because, as we said of acting and art as a whole, it is hard to reduce it to terms other than its own. The overt team-work of nicely dovetailed speech and movement is a matter of skill and practice easily appraised. What is not is the dialogue left unspoken, and the larger, the psychological structure of the play. For every ten lines the dramatist writes that the actors are to speak he may leave a hundred unwritten. If he did not confine himself to setting down the essential and significant only his play would never be finished. But the purport of what stays unwritten the actor, at his task, must nevertheless be able to divine; this is not so much rejected matter as scaffolding used for the play's building, to be discarded on its completion. Actors, preparing their performance, are, in a way, repeating that process, our students a part of it likewise. Therefore they must divine what it was (an aspect, this, of their collaboration with the author), and by some means agree upon it among themselves (their collaboration with each other). In all highly organized drama the amount of the unwritten will exceed the amount written by much; so the field in which the actors' imagination can operate will be wide. And in this, perhaps, the technique of the theatre reaches its maturest development, the art of the actor most fruitfully supplementing the dramatist's art. The actor interprets, and, as in any partnership, honesty of purpose is presumed. But the dramatist learns to give the actor material so contrived that only wilfully can he *mis*interpret it; and, for the rest, he leaves him free—he encourages him—to enrich his interpretation to the full extent of his own imaginative power.

Creative interpretation, self-expression to the full with the 'self' sacrificed; these paradoxes resolved, add a common loyalty to the play, coupled with loyalty to each other, and the actors' charter is complete. Again, the loyalty is currently little noted; but the taking it for granted, both by actors and audience, may be the best compliment that either could pay it. The actors of the chief parts have the play's fortunes in their hands, each other's fortunes too; and the actors of the least conspicuous parts, by the slightest lapse from loyalty, can do it disproportionate damage. Seldom or never is there any such lapse. They all combine to build a structure of mutual understanding and trust. And it is to more than play-acting, I repeat, that these principles of play-acting can be made to apply.

THE CASTING OF A PLAY: AMONG ACTORS; AMONG STUDENTS

Classwork, we said, which is in its nature co-operative, suits the co-operative nature of the drama well. And in studying a play it will obviously be convenient, at some time, to distribute its parts among the students very much as they are cast among a company of actors. But not wholly: the difference of aim—for the student no performance being in prospect—will demand a readjustment of method in more than one respect. It may be better not to give a student such entire possession of a part as an actor is given. For one reason, proprietary care of it may weaken his interest in the play as a whole; for another, if it is a small part, he may be wearied of it before the play as a whole can have been fully studied. A simple and obvious plan with plays of such a multitude of characters as have (for instance) *Antony and Cleopatra* or *Peer Gynt* would be to allot the longer parts singly and the shorter ones in bunches, or to ring the changes on them among the less advanced students. But there is something to be said—our purpose being pure study—for ridding the student altogether of this sense of property in a part, big or small.

For there remains the capital difference (already noted) between the actor's self-surrender, pending from the start, and the student's sustained detachment. Yet (also noted) this latter is to be no mere bookish understanding of the play but a lively appreciation of it too; and there can be more than one way of gaining that. It will depend on the dispositions of the student. To one the analytical approach will be easy. Trait by trait he will uncover and be ready to defend to the rest of the class the character of his Hamlet, Oedipus, or John Gabriel Borkman. Another student may go to work in quite another way, but one equally legitimate; first identifying himself intuitively with the character, then proceeding by argument and illustration to justify his intuition. Such a student may even wish to stop short of the argument, protesting that to put his deeply felt appreciation into words—mere words!—will only coarsen it. But his class-fellows have their right to argument and explanation. They are not to be content with his assurance that he inwardly knows just how Macbeth feels at that moment: can't they tell this by the very way he speaks the lines? Then he'll speak them again. And so he does *ad libitum*, and we are no further on. Therefore to reconcile the diversely gifted students, the quick in perception but weak in argument with the logically minded, I should be disposed, were I conducting such a class, to put parts which invited much discussion into commission, as it were. I would sooner have, not one Hamlet or one Iago, but three. As the old rhyme runs, 'One to watch and one to pray, and one to keep the Devil away'. The Devil in this case can safely be identified with the spirit sure to enter into some student in such a class, convincing him that Macbeth is Bothwell, or Hamlet a portrait of the Earl of Essex, Claudius of Leicester, Gertrude of Queen Elizabeth, and Ophelia of the Dark Lady; any excuse for talking such nonsense seeming sometimes to be better than none, with the best part of the hour wasted in escaping from the silly tangle. Let us note in passing that the work of the class, since it is not to reach the solidity of action, should be only the more securely anchored to common sense.[1] A play is in its nature a business of make-believe; and one degree of make-believe—a single thickness of fiction—is all that it will effectively carry.

To this point of likeness, then, and with this main difference, should we cast a play for study as for stage. For certain complex characters, better the convinced advocate than the would-be actor, who will only feel baffled when he is stopped short of acting. I should be anxious too—were I conducting such a class—to leave the less histrionically equipped students at no disadvantage.

THE 'EXPLICIT' AND 'IMPLICIT' METHODS OF PLAY-WRITING

Take next the question of more and less suitable material for our study. There are roughly—considering both to-day's and

[1] There would need to be also, I think, a running record kept of the progress of the class. Some sub-professor or super-student should at short intervals summarize the work done and the consensus of opinion reached (reservations noted) upon the more important issues that have come up for discussion: *e.g.* how much knowledge or suspicion has Gertrude of Claudius' guilt, and how much of this should—or can—the actress show? Is Lady Macbeth's swoon upon Macbeth's too glib account of his killing of the grooms who are to be saddled with the murder of Duncan genuine or a trick to take attention from him? What are we meant to gather in *Rosmersholm* of Rebecca West's relations to the dead Dr. West, what *do* we gather, and how is the scant material that Ibsen gives us here to be treated? It should be a business-like record, not aspiring to any literary style. It should primarily aim at reminding the class continually of the play's purport, and at keeping us conscious of its form. For this finds expression mainly in its action; and our restraint from that will leave us the more dangerously free to talk at large, saying, no doubt, many smart and illuminating things *about* the play, but not identifying ourselves with it closely enough. Authors of every sort are subject to the weakness, which lets them set out to write about one thing and go on writing about another. It is a weakness that the discipline of the dramatic form helps to correct. And equally in merely studying a play it is as well to keep on the narrow track.

yesterday's—two methods of play-writing, that demanding explicit interpretation, and that in which much of the meaning is left implicit, to be conveyed by the actors, not in words nor even in very forthright action, but largely by demonstrating the sort of pattern made in the relations and attitude of the characters toward each other and in the contrasts between them, the dialogue stressing the significance of the design. Marlowe's, for an example, is wholly 'explicit' drama, as is more primitive drama than his. So are Shakespeare's earlier plays, and his method in general remains throughout as explicit as the nature of play or character will allow it to be. Chekov's method, on the other hand, and in quite another fashion Maeterlinck's or Yeats', are 'implicit' in the extreme. Yet it is not a difference between modern drama and old. No dramatist could be more explicit than is Bernard Shaw, and others have been returning lately to old forms, while not half the significance in *King Lear* and *Macbeth* finds its way into plain words. But, speaking generally, it is the increased use of the implicit in drama which has marked its more modern developments ('modern' for me, I fear, meaning Ibsen and Chekov and Maeterlinck; my junior listeners must apply some other epithet), and the demands made on the actors have so far developed as to have all but changed. Romeo and Juliet, for instance, can be acted by a couple of children if they can speak and move as aptly as well-trained choir boys can sing (Shakespeare's Juliet, of course, was so acted, and nobody now thinks of commiserating him upon that; I have even heard him envied). So, indeed, can such a comparatively 'implicit' play as *Macbeth* be. In default of great acting for it, simple acting will suffice; impersonal, plastically pleasing, showing as much regard as possible for Shakespeare's share in the business and as little for the actor's own. The tragedy will still yield as much, and its better part. But in Chekov's *The Cherry Orchard*, unless the actress of Madame Ranevsky brings to her performance not only all she is directed to say and do, but something besides that she must pervasively and expressively *be* (and the same thing will be true and truer of acting in the later plays of that both 'explicit' and 'implicit' dramatist Ibsen), there will be left in the place the character should fill nothing but a very large hole. In most sorts of drama the actor's personality, animating and clothing the figure the dramatist has designed, will be a legitimate factor (if only, as we said, the distinction can be kept between personality manifested and ego exploited). But in this 'implicit' sort it is positively needed, and the art of the dramatist provides for and demands it. And this, in turn, calls on all that is maturest in the art of the actor. He may need to spend a professional lifetime making himself into an instrument that, for the dramatist's benefit, he can so sensitively play upon.

Little or nothing is to be gained from fully filled-in student performances of this implicit drama, from a Rebecca West or Hedda Gabler acted by—to put it unkindly, as we soon should—precocious schoolgirls, or from a Master Builder listening for the younger generation knocking at the door played by one of that very generation, vaultingly ambitious. On the other hand, the student, remaining a student, nor trying to reach to more than the fullest intellectual and emotional appeciation of it of which he is naturally capable, will be less at a disadvantage with this sort of play, however inadequate his powers over the *expression* of it may be; since—whether for student or actor—there is the more work to be done at it before putting it into action, and that dividing line can therefore be drawn the later. Our class can, in fact, very profitably *study* a play which they could not hope to *perform* with much benefit to themselves or pleasure to anybody else.

THE CO-OPERATIVE TASK

Their first step in their co-operative task will be to come to a common understanding of the play, complete enough, at any rate, to be workable. Of what we are to mean by 'workable' take this example. Hedda Gabler kills herself. There may be much difference of opinion in the class—most importantly between the two or three students who have been appointed 'counsel' for Hedda—as to precisely why she did so; still, as long as it is recognized that she would have done so, the incident remains workable. But Judge Brack, it will be remembered, that apostle of the polite conventions, cries out when the fatal shot is heard: 'God help us: people don't *do* these things.'   And if we think—to put it so—that the play *he* might have written about her (the play which he was so ready to act out in life), with its happy ending in adultery, would be the likelier one, why, there is plainly an *unworkable* difference of opinion between us and Ibsen himself. Then we must either begin to study her again or condemn the dramatist for inconsistency and weakness for a startling 'curtain'. And that, I remind you, we are, as students, quite at liberty to do, indeed, honestly bound to do; although as actors, set to perform the play, and about to identify ourselves with the characters, we soon should not be.

A common understanding must be reached as to the main lines of the action of the play. Even though our students are not to put it into action they must still imagine this rightly done. With the average play of to-day or yesterday, written for a familiar form of theatre, few questions, it may be said, can arise on this score, since the dramatist will usually have made plain what he wants done. But when a play was written for a theatre which is now *un*familiar—as Sheridan's is somewhat, Molière's rather more, Shakespeare's much more, the

Greek theatre wholly—and when moreover, as will then generally be the case, its action must be deduced from the framework of its speech only, which was all the dramatist considered needed writing down for his interpreters at the time; why, this leaves room for conjecture, and discussion is needed. The movements of the chorus in the *Agamemnon*, supplementing those of the characters on the stage, the marching and countermarching of the armies in *Antony and Cleopatra* and *Coriolanus*, these, and other such combinations of structure and action, are integral parts of the play. And, studying it, since we are not to see them, we must keep them only the more vividly in our mind's eye, or they will continually tend to fall back again and be re-absorbed into that sparsely printed page from which our imagination has had to evoke them.

The structure of the 'explicit' play—its action so clearly supplementing its speech, its speech explaining its action—cannot be hard to discern. Its qualities will lie in a well-told story that is worth telling, in a balancing of interests and the contrasting of the characters; for the rest, in such poetic rhetoric, it may be, as Hotspur's, in Falstaff's robust or Rosalind's lively prose, or in that of Eliot's chastened writing, or of Shaw's masterly eloquence. The worth or shortcomings of the story-telling, its balances and contrasts, ask no special knowledge for their demonstrating. The proof of such speech doubtless lies best in its speaking; and the essentials of that art are, as we said, properly to be learnt at an earlier than college age. But, granted some equipment in them, the student will often be able to bring to the 'explicit' play's demands in this kind a freshness of response which the over-practised actor may have lost. And if he does not, even should he be able to exhibit at this stage no more than a token value of (say) Hotspur's spirited defence of the withholding of the prisoners, or the Inquisitor's speech in Shaw's *Joan of Arc*, so long as it is enough for evidence that he *appreciates* their quality, the educational loss will not be great.

THE STUDY OF A PLAY PUTS ITS TECHNIQUE ON TRIAL

The classwork by which the students will test and augment their own knowledge necessarily becomes also something like a test and trial of the play itself. We consider this first as a whole. Though it may seldom be planned in any strict obedience to the famous Unities, some sort of unity it must have. An approximate unity of subject will be convenient, if the attention of an audience is to be happily held, and a unity of convention, for the sustaining of the make-believe. But the conditions of the theatre positively force on the drama certain limiting disciplines. The actors—for a dominating instance —are physically limited in what they can do; and this human medium affects all that touches it. The dramatist will not employ his scenic conventions in a fashion which they, the actors, cannot make convincing. Shakespeare inherits in his theatre, with its platform stage and illocalized balconies and curtains, a seemingly untrammelled freedom in space and time, and his audience would customarily yield to his suggestions a most obedient imagination. But, with his extraordinary 'sense of the theatre', he never taxes this aimlessly or too far, never leaves us questioning. Convention in the theatre is a gentleman's agreement between dramatist, actors, and audience. It involves (as do all agreements) consistency, and consideration in the use of it. Shakespeare retains the scenic freedoms of his bare stage, but he uses them considerately. Ibsen, writing for his theatre of scenic illusion, has surrendered them, has, so to put it, anchored himself in space, and, more closely than any of his predecessors, in time. And he cannot arbitrarily resume his freedom. He makes a half-attempt to do so in his last two plays; when John Gabriel Borkman sets off up the snow-bound mountain, in the ending of *When We Dead Awaken* amid avalanches and hymns to freedom. But this does not quite do. The agreement has been broken. The actors may not object to this incontinent reshaping of it; but we, the audience, having first accepted one sort of illusion, will be unwilling suddenly to change; and against our discomfort neither dramatist nor actors can successfully contend. Audience and actors must be at ease together.[1]

THE QUESTION OF DRAMATIC INTEGRITY

More vital, however, than consistency of convention will be the inner quality of dramatic integrity. A play, as we said, involves conflict, outward or inward; this keeps it alive. Its story will be told chiefly by the setting out of differences between the characters. The action develops these and will at last dispose of them, be it, as in comedy, by reconciliation

[1] It may be argued that an audience, having seen a play given on one night under conditions of scenic illusion, will accept without difficulty Shakespeare and his conventions the next. Yes; but until how recently has Shakespeare not been adapted to the conventions of the contemporary stage? To a degree he still is. To a degree it is because this is 'Shakespeare' that an intimidated audience will swallow his stagecraft (nearly) whole. There have lately been, it may be added, various experiments in convention. But they have remained experiments, no general change has developed from them; not, certainly, from one pseudo-Chinese production I remember, nor from a most delightful one out of two projected by Mr. Thornton Wilder. And I doubt whether, in any of the three instances, the parties to the business—author, actors, and audience—were wholly at their ease. A certain self-consciousness, an air of artificial innocence, pervaded it.

Of more importance is Mr. T. S. Eliot's recent *The Family Reunion*, with its modern treatment of the matter of a Greek tragedy. The conventions are mixed: but the actual inclusion of the Eumenides among the characters—mute, but visible both to hero and audience—is for me at once the unlikeliest and the least necessary of the devices. Mr. Eliot has not yet matured, I think, with perfect certainty, the visually imaginative side of his dramatic art. On the other hand, the verbal treatment of chorus and dialogue, the significant blending of realistic and formal, I find masterly indeed. And while it would be work, truly, for very advanced students, in a testing trial of this play, a distinguishing between its achievements and its shortcomings, we should be dealing with some of the fundamentals of drama.

and agreement or by tragic catastrophe—and there are variations enough between these two extremes. The thing to remember is that the differences must always be fairly fought
out, each character being allowed to say and do his best on his
own behalf. There must be no fraudulent tipping of the scales
by the dramatist in favour of this one or that, no lucky but too
unlikely accident occurring, no over-opportune conversions
from one opinion to another. For the fraud of these will be at
once detected, unless the audience is as gullible as the dramatist
is dishonest. And characters so indulged will at once lose their
dramatic integrity. They will forfeit their seemingly inde-
pendent status in that mimic world which we have agreed to
accept for an hour or so as the real world. At the sign of such
weakness, such a lapse into puppetdom, we in turn shall
weaken in our belief in it, and in them. And it is in this belief
—willingly accorded at first, yet to be lost all but unawares—
that the maturer art of the drama subsists.

Very much as we feel that a man may be called on to justify
his existence in the real world, so must a character's place,
speech, and actions in a play be justifiable. And the student
temporarily identifying himself with a character or given its
interest to defend, will have to make a case for them against
whatever devil's advocacy the rest of the class can muster. The
brief, on the face of it, may seem but a meagre one. What the
character does and says in the short course of the play, what is
said *to* the character, what *about* it—in strictness that can be
all; and except possibly for certain forms of poetry there is no
thriftier kind of writing than the dramatic. A stock curiosity
in my youth was the Lord's Prayer written on a threepenny
piece. In such a script the whole of Lady Macbeth could, I
suppose, be accommodated on a silver dollar, and Hamlet—
the part if not the play—on the front and back of a dollar bill.
And Shakespeare's was a comparatively verbose school of
writing—'explicit' we have called it—delighting in words and

their beauty. He had, moreover, to suggest in words such scenery as he might think the play needed, a background for its action; and in every play time must be spared in which to tell the audience all that needs to be known of what has happened before the action begins, in providing it, so to say, with the background of its past; this, from the very little time available. There are simple ways of building up this past, be it of the play as a whole or of a single character; by the Prologue—nothing could be simpler—bringing the story to the point at which the action begins and can, in the present tense and unencumbered, carry it on; by narrative —a little less simple this—embodied in the action, shaped, perhaps, as reminiscences exchanged between the characters. Familiar devices range from *Romeo and Juliet's* 'Two houses both alike in dignity . . .' to the opening of almost any nineteenth-century French farce with its valet and chambermaid, and their 'Didn't Master get home very late last night? . . .' [1] But the student will find that, as the art of the drama matures, his brief for a character is reduced more to the dimensions and the stuff of the character itself.

IBSEN AND HIS 'ROSMERSHOLM'

Turn to Ibsen, that artist and craftsman combined; not the Ibsen of the history plays, nor of *Brand* and *Peer Gynt*, but the Ibsen who protests he has forsworn the poetic drama— though in truth he had only found out how to write it in prose. His technical aim now is to make his play's action and his characters as self-explanatory as possible; and what needs

---

[1] For the classic burlesque of this method see, of course, Sheridan's *The Critic*; Sir Walter Raleigh to Sir Christopher Hatton: 'You know, my friend, scarce two revolving suns . . . You know, besides . . . You also know . . .' and so on, until Dangle interrupts with 'But, Mr. Puff, as he knows all this, why does Sir Walter go on telling him?' to be snubbed by a 'But the audience are not supposed to know anything of the matter, are they?' Not such sheer burlesque, either!

to be known of the past will be brought out in terms of its interest to the present. For the present tense is the dramatic tense. A play's dialogue is a species of conflict, sportive or bitter, usually a series of duels varied by more general fighting. The mere looking backwards of narrative or reminiscence will soon slacken our interest; it is at best as if the combatants were resting between bouts to exchange memories of past fighting. Ibsen aims also at giving his characters that seeming independence of the author, of which we spoke, for an attribute to their dramatic integrity; and to do this he sacrifices the convenient and time-honoured devices of the aside and soliloquy, by which their intimate thoughts and feelings could be directly revealed to the audience. Shakespeare's stage had few scenic furnishings; Ibsen in turn strips his of all such conventions as these. So little is there in his dialogue to remind us of the theatre that we seem less to be hearing these conversations from our stalls than privately *over-hearing* them.

Yet this talk, which will seem not meant for our ears, is to be made to bring us into as close a touch with *Rosmersholm's* Rebecca West as his soliloquies, all but addressed to us, bring Hamlet; the very souls of the Rita and Alfred Allmers of *Little Eyolf* are to be laid bare to us, and to themselves. Here is the paradox of great drama. This most physical of the arts becomes, in the hands of its masters, one of the choicest vehicles for inward revelation, yet still, thanks to the familiarity of its human medium, the most convincing. Ibsen's problem in plays of the *Rosmersholm* technique is, while keeping the talk just such as the immediate occasion would produce, to fill it besides with all else that the play's working out demands; and every passage of the dialogue will be put to double—sometimes, indeed, to triple—use. It must advance the actual action, revealing the character of the speakers as it does so. It may show us the character of the

listeners also, by their mute response—or lack of response—
to it. And bit by bit, the delays increasing our suspense,
the story of the past comes out; of Rebecca's crime, of how
ruthlessly she lured the unhappy Beata to suicide, so that, she
told herself, Rosmer might be spiritually free. And this builds
up the never-seen Beata's character too. Further, into the
unornamented talk and the few simple comings and goings
of the action—Rosmer's slow, haunted movements, Rebecca's
quiet tread, Madam Helseth's pleasant homeliness for contrast—there is woven a picture of Rosmersholm itself. Not
descriptively, in competition with scene-painting and car-
pentry. We have the *atmosphere* of the old house, in which
children neither laugh nor cry (says Madam Helseth), with
its traditions of conformity and order, its mill-race thundering
without, and the legend of the White Horses. Time is even
found for a few words about the pugnacious Rector Kroll's
domestic troubles, for a glimpse into Mortensgård's scandal-
dogged past, for twin flashes across the scene of the tragi-
comic idealist Ulric Brendel. And these strokes of a picture
of what is happening *around* Rosmersholm, reflected from what
is happening *within* Rosmersholm, make this the more vivid.

For it all contributes to the main action of the play, which
is the spiritual tragedy of Rosmer and Rebecca, with its dis-
coveries and disclosures and their consequences. Rebecca has
learnt of herself, since she began to gather in the harvest of
her ill-doing, that her motives for it were not so noble as she
liked to think; of Rosmer she learns that he is not the man to
profit by freedom even ignorantly so gained. He discovers
that he loves her and has always loved her. But it is with a
love that has transformed—*she* discovers—her passion for
him into a like love, which will not let her profit by her sin.
And instead of freeing his mind from its trammels she has
only taught him to despair; while he has taught her to take
the 'Rosmersholm' view of life, which demands atonement

for sin. Finally, to be free of this wreck of their beliefs, the tangle of doubt, the intolerable strain, they go to their death together by the way the wronged Beata went. And the old servant cries out as she sees it, 'The dead wife has taken them!'

That is a poor enough epitome of the two hours of over-heard talk (itself a masterpiece of condensation) which is the total matter of the play. Ibsen's usual two years of brooding work went to its writing; and our class could, I think, give it a fair number of hours of study without milking it dry of interest, technical and metaphysical too. There are only six characters, and two of them have no more than a passing concern with the story; but two at least—Rebecca most certainly —are many-faceted enough in their showing to invite more than one approach, provide for ample discussion; and their dramatic integrity will stand the test of the closest analysis. *Rosmersholm*, moreover, is the kind of play (there are not many of its kind and quality combined, by Ibsen or anybody else!) which can be made to yield the most to sheer study, in which the lack of physical action, so little is there, will leave the least lacking. And in that it will meet our class's demands.

But it is an exciting play too. It is a spiritual detective story. The facts of Rebecca's crime come out easily enough; and they are all that would have interested the commonplace dramatist, or would appeal, supposedly, to a commonplace audience.[1] More interesting are the motives; that is true of any crime. And it is out of the complex of these, gradually disentangled and revealed, that the pattern of the past—of the derivative action, so to call it—is assembled for us. But

[1] There was, indeed, in London at the time of the play's first production there, a gentleman who wrote under the name of Austin Fryers, and who—contending that Ibsen had missed the true point of his own work—perpetrated a sort of pro-logue to it, which he called *Beata*, in which he dealt with her side of the story, setting out in three—doubtless very lively—acts the matter which the dunder-headed Norwegian had compressed into four or five reminiscent speeches, for use merely as the seed of his evolved tragedy of character.

most gripping of all are the accumulating consequences of these revelations to the human souls concerned. The play's essential action—its present tense—is in these. And it throws a light into the very depths of man's nature and upon some of the mysteries that lie there.

Ibsen draws no moral. Even as for the telling of the story and the unfolding of character he has discarded soliloquy, aside, and every other such open acknowledgment of his audience, so now—all said and done that need be—he brings the play to an uncommented end.[1] For the dramatist's business is not to moralize, but simply to see that—as to a question asked—his play tells the truth in reply, and that it is a significant truth, worth the telling. And our business in studying drama is to cultivate, to sharpen and refine, our hearing and appreciation until we can swiftly distinguish between what is significant and truly told, and what, in a poor play, is neither. And—yet once more—this is a very educative exercise.

BUT STUDY LEAVES THE PLAY, AS IT FINDS IT, A WORK OF ART

The 'overheard' play such as *Rosmersholm*—with its compacted story asking all attention and its complex of emotions painfully unravelling—offers much to the student even in demanding much from him, and more than a lesson in stage-craft. For the art of the dramatist presents it very nearly as the matter of it might present itself in life; and such self-identifying study of it as we have in mind will all but measure up to an experience undergone. And from this our student may emerge, if not a little wiser than he was—wisdom comes

---

[1] The precisian may object that Madam Helseth's closing outburst is both comment and soliloquy. The answer to this can be that under great stress of emotion people do so exclaim out loud, to themselves, and sometimes in turned sentences too. If that is not acceptable let us say that Ibsen was too experienced a dramatist not to know when he could advantageously break his own rules.

more slowly—at least a little keener in discerning the things about him. Rebecca's case, it may be said, is not a common one. There will not, it is fairly certain, be any young woman listening to me to-night with a Beata for a rival, set to be rid of her—and with a mill-stream handy too! Yet one never knows. As Grant Allen said when the critics of fifty years ago cried out on Hedda Gabler as a quite 'impossible' character, 'Nonsense; I take her down to dinner once a week.' There will not be in my audience, for that matter, many young men whose uncles have murdered their fathers and debauched their mothers, but there will be few who have not found themselves faced at some time, in one form or another, with some of Hamlet's moral problems. To which point I will return later.

Finally, however, we must never let our study of a play discount its value to us as a work of art. We pull it to pieces for educational use very much as actors do in rehearsing it, with this chief difference, that we do not have to consider putting it together again, as they must, for the performance which will complete and justify its existence. Our students will not possess the special skill for that or be equipped to acquire it; nor, then, will they wisely wish to exchange the student's critical for the actor's devoted attitude. For, having well studied a play, they really should have gained too much regard for it to be ready to defame it by a crude performance. But such students will make the best possible audience for the best possible performance of it that can be given. And they will have earned the right to this. How it is to be provided for them is another question.

III

A Theatre That Might Be

PATRONAGE AND CENSORSHIP

We spoke, in passing, of the effects of patronage upon
the various British arts. Upon that of the drama they
have been peculiar. It was, so to say, bred, if not born, in
patronage. The early companies of actors were known as the
King's Men, the Queen's, the Lord Chamberlain's, the Lord
Admiral's Men; and without some such badge of protection
they could not follow their calling, but were liable to arrest
as 'rogues and vagabonds'.[1] For those were still the days in
England when a man had to 'belong' somewhere, to be a
recognized part of the body politic. When the Puritans came
into power both plays and players were summarily suppressed;
and, when the King's restoration permitted theirs, it was, as
with other things, under less feudal conditions. The sovereign,
through the Lord Chamberlain, had the customary power of
licensing or disallowing all dramatic performances; and
Charles II now gave 'patents' to two of his courtiers,
privileging them to muster two companies and build two
theatres. And he gave each of them besides the exclusive
rights to a long list of plays—Shakespeare's were divided
between them—which, by our modern notions of property,
were not his to give. But it was effective patronage—as far
as it went. And it went thus much further, that he was
himself an assiduous playgoer. I only hope he paid for his
seats (I do not know; there is a point in theatrical history
which it behoves some student to investigate). That, at any

---

[1] I believe this to have been the only practical application in their case of that
much quoted phrase.

rate, was as far as it did go. And ever since 'patronage' of the theatre, whether by kings or lesser folk, has commonly meant this and little more.[1]

The power of the royal prerogative has by now diminished to a shadow, except in the matter of the licensing of plays; and there it is still solid enough, though it may be more timidly handled than it was. But within my own recollection it proved a mischievous clog upon what looked to be a very promising renaissance of the English drama. The positive harm done may not have seemed great, the forbidding the public stage to a dozen plays or so: *The Cenci, Ghosts, Monna Vanna, Mrs. Warren's Profession, Les Avariés, La Citta Morta,* and some by lesser men. There was no 'money' in any of them (as the theatre counts money to-day), nor the making of a procession or a riot or a Trafalgar Square meeting as a protest against their suppression. I remember the Home Secretary of that day telling me privately that if we organized a protest of sufficient violence to make the Government uncomfortable—why, something might be done. But otherwise, to expect that cabinet of Liberal Ministers to add even such a trifle as this, quite gratuitously, to their many weightier troubles, showed, on my part, a regrettable innocence. Did I, at a time when Home Rule, a 'People's Budget' and the Parliament Act were looming, expect them to lay a finger upon one of the few remaining—and politically quite harmless —odds and ends of royal authority? To this day the Lord Chamberlain's powers over the theatre are little less despotic than they were in Queen Elizabeth's reign. They are at one

---

[1] Readers of *Nicholas Nickleby* will remember Miss Snevellicci's bespeak, Mr. Curdle on the unities of the drama, and the three half-crowns. ' And ', said Miss Snevellicci, ' I assure you . . . that I think myself very lucky they did not owe all the money instead of being sixpence short. Now, if you were to succeed, they would give people to understand that they had always patronized you; and if you were to fail, they would have been quite certain of that from the very beginning.' But there has been generous patronage of the drama in England as well as mean, generous, and extravagant; little that has been both generous and wise.

with other timeworn traditions that the English lovingly cling
to—the Woolsack, the ceremonies in Parliament, the state
coach with its eight cream-coloured ponies, the Beefeaters,
and the rest of the trappings. I cling to them myself when
the price to be paid in realities is not too high.[1] But here it is
so; for drama should be something more than an amusing
pageant. And the price paid has been not less than the degrada-
tion of its entire status. The drama has been compulsorily
patronized; but with this has gone no obligation on the part
of the patron to support it. In other countries, kings admitted one and the governments that replaced them assumed
it. The theatre became a recognized public institution. See
how the French people, with France at her poorest, would
receive a serious proposal to abolish the *Comédie Française*.
A few years ago an act of gross contempt for its administration
was worth a very black mark indeed against the Minister
responsible. But in England and (originally by example) in
the United States too its status is merely commercial.

THE 'COMMERCIAL' THEATRE

Now, by that it has in the past earned a certain respect,
the respect which a self-supporting industry can always
claim, on this ground if no other. And, during these latter
years, treaty-making with cinema and radio has brought
much extra prosperity to actor, director, and dramatist according to the popularity they have achieved; and to the financiers,
the money-spinners who exploit them, probably even more.
Well, it is idle to condemn success; nor need one as long as it
is clear under what conditions the success is gained and what
the sequel is likely to be. But more and more it looks as if,
under these, the drama, properly so called, were forfeiting its

[1] The ponies have, indeed, not been heard of lately. Are they out to grass
at last ?

independence, losing its peculiar quality, and might sink into place as one of the pettier parts of a gigantic entertainment industry, to the demands of which it must obediently adapt itself. It is at present bargaining for its livelihood. It still has prestige to sell—mostly associated with the personality of a few favourite actors and actresses—but the competitive value of even this is, I fear, diminishing. And I do not think that a summary of the fortunes—and misfortunes—of the New York theatre, which I happened to see in some newspaper and note at the finish of its last season, is evidence to the contrary. This records the staging of seventy-three plays and more. A 'success' may have registered some two thousand consecutive performances. A so-called failure will have been shoved out of the way as quickly as possible; its losses cut. A play is said to do good or bad 'business', it makes or loses money, that is to say; and there is no other yardstick of success and failure. But is this popular verdict a really satisfactory measure of the *quality* of a play? Can profit and loss to the *art* of the drama be properly estimated in such terms?

A conspicuous place in the present record falls to the two million and a half dollars worth of 'screen sales' made. A satisfactory item, no doubt, to those that pocket the money, but of a very indirect benefit to the drama. A detailed balance sheet of the financing of the New York theatre industry, closely analysed, would be an illuminating document. And we should see a picture, I suppose, of what a banker or lawyer might possibly consider financial disorder—out of which, nevertheless, a skilful operator in this market, careful to keep hold of the thick end of the stick (that being the ownership of those strange and uncomfortable buildings in which plays are performed), manages to fish a steady little profit year by year. The sponsors of the plays gamble more headily. As to the actors and directors, while the sun of a 'success' shines, they make all the hay they can; when it stops shining they must be ready to pack up quick and seek better weather elsewhere. It may be, of course, that this queer combination of usury and gambling, this general irresponsibility, suits the drama well enough, since it is, in some aspects, the most volatile and ephemeral of the arts. Is not, therefore, the true spirit of it best fostered in happy-go-lucky, shiftless levity? Thespis and his cart, Hogarth's strolling players in their barn, Mr. Vincent Crummles and the Infant Phenomenon—there was a lot of fun in them; and every now and then an Edmund Kean would come tramping through the mud. But, alas, the simplicity and innocence of this seem gone beyond recall; and there is something incongruously vulgar about a bank account in Bohemia.

WHAT IS A THEATRE?

The four-hundred-year history of the English-speaking theatre shows one or two short periods in which companies of actors working loyally together did their calling some credit, and, beside these, a number of notable individual careers. For the rest, it is a record of episode after episode, all to a pattern; of passing triumphs, and disasters forgotten, storms in teacups, vanities displayed and tempers lost, much dull daily work honestly done and ignored, and—alack and inevitably— much ploughing of the sands. But it is ill belabouring the people of the theatre for their human frailties, which differ most from those of other people in being easier to advertise. What history must ask of any theatre is chiefly this: has it, throughout the years, done well and worthily by the drama given into its charge?

In view of its difficulties, 'Not so badly' is, I suppose, a fair answer. True, we English have no House of Shakespeare, as the French have their House of Molière, which is besides, of course, a home—if a not too accommodating one—for

Corneille, Racine, Victor Hugo, Rostand, Becque, some of whose work at least it is charged to keep alive (incidentally it has become of late years a Parisian *pied-à-terre* for Shakespeare). We English-speaking peoples have a *drama*—a four-hundred-year accumulation of it—outranked by none in the world; and, thanks to recurring spells of enthusiasm, backed often by preposterous self-sacrifice, this has so far managed to rally time and again, even from its worst doldrums. But we have no such *theatre*. Why not? In England itself the truth-fullest answer to this as to similar questions would simply be: because so far we never have had. But that is no answer in the United States; the best of reasons, rather, for having one if other reasons are good. No such theatre! And, it can be added, nothing in any English-speaking country that is properly to be called a theatre at all. A man I knew long ago had passed the most energetic years of his life creditably and successfully in various theatrical pursuits; and he suddenly vanished from those scenes. I asked him when I met him some time later, 'Why did you leave the theatre?' He answered me, 'Because there was none to leave'.

By 'theatre' he evidently did not mean, then, merely one of those buildings in which a scratch company of actors can be assembled and a play rehearsed and performed time after time to a casual crowd at so much a head until the immediate demand for it is exhausted. For a true theatre a building is needed, certainly, even as is a factory for the manufacture of motor-cars or fountain-pens, and the better equipped the factory, the more efficient and economical the manufacture will be. But by a theatre (he explained) he meant rather, and before all, a stable organization of actors and actresses and director-producers and designers, an institution in which the whole art of the drama could be cultivated for its own sake and made manifest. There would be performances, of course; an audience is a necessary sounding-board for a play. And this audience had better as a matter of form be let pay something for their seats; they will—such is human nature—value them the more, and so not conduct themselves toward the institution too casually. But performances—more particularly crowded performances—would not be the sole test of the theatre's utility. The numbers in which people came to contrasted plays would be for the management a current test of the relations between the theatre and its public, simply that. For those must be kept healthy and friendly; no institution can properly exist to itself alone. But plays would no more be performed in such a theatre for the *sole* purpose of attracting a crowd than a Flemish primitive will be bought or rejected by the Metropolitan Museum here in New York upon the taking of a city-wide plebiscite (the time may come when the public taste will be so reliable, but it has not come yet), or than a public librarian will timidly fill his shelves with little but best-sellers.

The parallel between such a theatre and museum or library cannot be exact since their economy differs so widely. A picture may be put on pretty permanent exhibition, a play cannot be; and while a single reader can be allowed to take from its shelf a book that he wants, the manager of the theatre must feel convinced that a certain number of people, at any rate, will be attracted by the play (even if patience be needed) before he sets in motion the somewhat complex machinery for putting it on the stage. But the relation of all three institutions to the public, and the services that those working in them may render to art and literature and drama, will in essence be very much the same. A good library will aim at stocking its shelves with as many as may be of the representative books of the world, a good picture gallery at possessing representative specimens of painting. Does the library, incidentally, compete unfairly, or at all, with the bookseller? No; it encourages people to read and even buy books they might never have chosen for themselves. Indirectly, picture galleries help to sell other pictures to those who have there learnt to like painting. Music needs foresighted organization and endowment, so by now it seems to be agreed, if we are to have other than catchpenny music. The drama depends more upon organization than does any other art. Is it to be the only one left wholly to the higgling of the market?

If a graph could be drawn of the fortunes of the theatre in England it is the first fifty years or so of its history that would show the sharpest ascent. Then comes the Puritan break; after its mending, fortuitous ups and downs, periods of credit and of more or less discredit. Already, at the end of the seventeenth century, the author of *Historia Histrionica* is lamenting the good old days of the King's Company, headed by those 'grave and sober men, living in reputation'. Later come Garrick, the Kembles, Macready, Irving, Booth; brilliant, and of their sort, imposing figures. But they and the rest all pass, leaving only memories behind them. This has been counted an inevitable limitation of the actor's art; those belittling it kindly allowing the extravagant applause it sometimes earns to be but fair compensation for the unkindness. Is the future to be otherwise? The last few years with their inventions have raised the question. Are the screen and the record to combine henceforth to confer a sort of mechanical immortality upon the actor?

THE MOVIE

These inventions—it is possible—are as yet in their infancy only. Science even now offers us, for the turning of a switch, the voice of a singer, the sound of an orchestra—and whether it is the voice of the dead or the living, whether the music is being made now while we listen or was recorded years ago, who is to tell? Every movie we see and hear, however new, is still a record of the past; whether it was taken a month or ten years back will soon make little difference. And we are promised a perfecting of television, which will certainly be susceptible of record too; so that a man may sit at home before his own silver screen and switch on the picture of his choice; not merely the latest thing, but, if he is in the mood, that which once charmed him, when the stars that shone in it shone more refulgently than they could do to-day (wisely retired upon their savings, he will trust). And except for the relief simply of going out and getting away from home—an important factor, however, this!—here is one likely prospect for the great entertainment industry. Its products will be brought to our doors with the milk and the groceries. And if the traditional, old-fashioned drama comes to selling itself yet more extensively for a well-paid petty share in this, it can look, of course, to a similar prospect. And why should it not? Why (it will then be asked) put up these cumbrous and costly buildings and mobilize actors in them night after night to parrot a play through, when science enables us, after taking all the pains needed to prepare the best performances possible —a single one sufficing—to record it and preserve it? Until now, the finest performances of the greatest plays have been condemned to share the human mortality of the actors that animate them. The marvellous movie has shown us, surely, a better way. Let us then have done with the theatre as we have known it and set to work accumulating libraries, visual and auditory, of records of the drama. The art of Titian, of Verrocchio, of Beethoven is thus preserved to us, and already the great musicians of to-day are more widely known by records than in person. Why should not the future Garrick or Kean be given just such immortality?

It sounds the right sort of thing for a scientific age. What would be wrong with it? I want to absolve myself from any suspicion of prejudice against the movie. I have never been concerned in making one; but I am a confirmed movie-goer, and have been so from the days of its restful silence (but for the buzzing of the projector and the anomalous clatter of the piano), those tentative days when movie-makers took plays for their models very much as the earliest railway builders made trains of horse-carriages fastened on trucks. Since then they have found their own formulas, and the technical advance has been amazing. The movie can, of course, do things that the theatre can never compass, and it is seen at its best, possibly, in doing them. The best movie-makers, I should suppose, think and plan chiefly in terms of pictures from the beginning. What is there, if anything, that the old-fashioned theatre can do and the movie cannot? And here, you may say, I am bound to be prejudiced. I learned to enjoy the theatre before the movie was born. The millions who now learn to enjoy the movie before ever they see a play acted—if they ever do—may equally be disappointed by the cramping conventions of the theatre. There is no absolute standard in such matters, and I do not attempt to dictate one. I can but note the effect made on me and do my best to explain it.

I find that what I look for and like best in the movie is technical achievement. Striking photography will do much to atone for the banality of the scenes photographed. But pleasure in spectacle is quickly gratified; and it is less readily renewable, one seldom wants to see a movie twice. The movie-maker seems to be for ever trying to reconcile his public's craze for novelty with the financial safety of the accustomed thing. And a craze for novelty will be the curse of any art. Now spectacle plays a small part in the theatre, for more than a modicum of it can only depreciate the actor's share in a play. It is in the actor and his acting that the pulse of the drama beats. If the movie, then, is to make the drama its own, it must do as well by the actor as the theatre has done. So far, of course, it has not; and to deny this is merely to show oneself insensible to what the actor—given opportunity—*can* do. To make him part of a picture, however cunningly our attention is focussed on that part, is to give him only the fraction of an opportunity. And 'registered' speech, assimilated to the picture, must surely be under like limitations. Machinery may capture the moment at its best both in sight and sound; but in doing this it stereotypes it, and robs the actor of his natural power over the audience. It comes to this, I think. Accomplishments and externals of all sorts can be reproduced; but the human factor in the theatre involves something more. Upon what does the *power* of the actor over his audience rest? For a very short while upon his looks, nor to a great extent upon how skilfully he does what he has to do. For longer, perhaps, on the magnetism of his speech. But ultimately it seems to rest upon something that he *is*. Other qualities may attract an audience, but it is by this that he will hold them. Can the movie find means then—as it must if it is to seize the theatre heritage—by which he can exercise this power to the full at second hand? That is the question.

THE ACTOR'S STANDPOINT

Actors at present will inevitably be most concerned with the ephemeral aspect of the drama, since their own stake in it, however distinguished, must be of this particularly mortal kind. The drama, complete in its acting, has more of the attributes of life itself than has any other art; and, like life, it passes. Yet even now there *is* another aspect: its unique credit as a co-operative art, still being built up over the years by the accumulation of a body of plays which have in them an enduring worth and vitality. But for these and the standard they set, the actor's art would still be abiding at about the level of the *commedia dell' arte*. It finds its higher ranges only in such plays as these. For a parallel, consider what the credit of a musician would be if he contented himself and thought to content his audience with nothing but the music that is written to-day mostly to be forgotten to-morrow.

A theatre—again, not a theatre building, but an organization by which the art of the drama can be cultivated—should enshrine these two aspects of it, of the plays to be performed, of the art of their presentation; and its value will lie in the reconciling of the two. Material equipment must be adequate, if only for economy's sake; but primarily it will be an association of men and women co-operating in the practice of an art. Discipline will be needed. In no comparable activity is it needed more. And nowhere, one may add, is discipline more likely to be found—despite vulgar report to the contrary—than in a well-organized theatre. But it must be self-discipline. For there is a danger in organizing any art, that of organizing the free spirit by which it lives—its peculiar virtue—out of existence altogether. One must beware of mere efficiency; a dead end. The aim here would be to develop in the theatre and its company that best sort of comradeship, which belongs to the good regiment, the good government, the good school or university, in which individual pride becomes pride in the whole, by which the value of the whole comes mysteriously to exceed that of the sum of the parts. And whenever this semi-miracle is achieved the effect will perhaps be more notable in a body of artists working happily together than in any other collection of fallible human beings.

THE DRAMA OF ENDURING WORTH

The main problem for such a theatre as we are envisaging (but it is the problem of all institutions) would lie in this combining of stability and vitality. Its stability would let it be in some sort a guardian of that drama of enduring worth upon which, as we said, the prestige of the art of the theatre ultimately rests. It could save plays of this quality from oblivion; its company of actors and producers would put their continuing vitality to the proof. It could enlarge the scope of the drama's general appeal, triply limited as this now is, by the sort of play acted, in the way it commonly is acted, in the narrow section of the public appealed to. Doubtless our purveyors of theatrical fare are ever assiduously seeking the 'new idea'—which to profit by need be neither so new nor very much of an idea—and variety at any cost. But when this is found it usually proves to be only superficial, shop-window variety, behind which the old monotony persists. The actors are still called on to sound—to a slightly different tune perhaps—the same few, well-worn notes, out of the wide gamut of expression that they could command: the comic, which 'gets a laugh', the erotic, the pathetic, which, dwelt on, earns an occasional sniff. If these are all to which the ear and the taste of an audience are attuned the rest may as well be left dumb. Why should an actor—and how can he!—cultivate to the fullest an art that he is only called on to exercise so crudely and scrappily? Let him follow where popularity leads and learn only what applause can teach him. He will be 'successful', that being his aim; but with half his capacities coarsened by over-use, and the rest atrophied for lack of any.

THE THEATRE'S THIRD FACTOR: THE AUDIENCE

As to the audience :

> The drama's laws the drama's patrons give,
> And we, who live to please, must please to live.

—upon which conventional, bowing and scraping compliment, the genus audience plumes itself to this day. But it is lickspittle doctrine, and likely to encourage—Johnson might, in a more serious moment, have stopped to consider—only such drama as he himself, from his seat in the pit, would have damned at sight. It is futile to appeal to public taste for a lead. That will lead nowhere, since the public has no taste—none more positive, or of better quality, at least, than is being currently taught it by dramatists and actors and ratified by a critic or two; and even so it arrives at nothing more specific than an unthinking Yes or No. There are various sorts of audience, yet not very variously composed. Hamlet and his kin have a place in some, and could re-write the play, and know just how it should be acted. Polonius will certainly be there. He, if you remember, did enact Julius Caesar in the university once; now, by the time we meet him, 'he is for a jig or a tale of bawdry, or he sleeps'. But appeal will be mainly made to the presumed majority, who expect entertainment and as much excitement as will digest their latest meal. Though there is nothing wrong about that, there comes to be about nothing but that; moreover, if the entertainer makes such entertainment his sole and direct aim, he grows, by over-confident repetition, likelier to miss than to hit it.

The pervading difficulty in the theatre lies in the close interdependence—in no co-operative art is this closer—of its several factors. A play must have a fitting company of actors; together they must have a fitting audience too. And these three factors—this is the crux of the matter—must find themselves in simultaneous and all but unanimous accord. A play may be appealing on any occasion but to a minority of its potential public, its actors cannot to a minority of a particular audience; they might be left acting, before the performance ended, to a minority of one—or less! To the enlarging of the scope of the drama, then, to an enhancing of its quality, all three factors must contribute, each as it can; and what one may try to do without the other two, or two without the third, will be largely wasted effort. So it has been. The history of the theatre, distant and recent, records a gallant and ever-hopeful succession of these transient or abortive efforts, soon forgotten, except by the theatrical historian, who must collect such uncertain memories of them as he may. Only the dramatist can in the nature of things leave some preciser record of his work behind him, his share in the whole, from which the whole—the play in complete being—can be brought to life again. We justly speak of 'reviving' a play.

THE PAST WHICH IS NO PAST

During the four hundred years and more of the modern drama's existence many plays of many sorts have been written. Most of them, no doubt, were—as most plays apparently ever are—imitations of imitations of what was not worth imitating to begin with, never had much more life in them than was given them by their first actors, and certainly would not respond to any attempt to revive them. Then there are the plays, still full enough of vitality, but only written to be of topical interest (though sometimes your author writes better than he knows). Are these worth reviving? Are they capable of real revival? Can we, with the best will in the world, come to appreciate the wit-combats of *Love's Labours Lost*? Luckily, we say, the speech about the King's Evil in *Macbeth* is easily omitted. Do we genuinely enjoy *Les Précieuses Ridicules*? How much do we not inevitably miss of the satire of *An Enemy of the People*?

But a very small change turns 'topical' into 'historical' interest, and that can be a positive addition to a play's value nowadays. Never, I suppose, has a sense of the past been more widely cultivated and under so many guises as in the last few decades. Various aspects of history, political, social, economic; biographies by the hundred; diaries; correspondence; facts fictionalized and frank fiction; centenaries celebrated weekly—have we ever shown such interest in our ancestors before? It is easily explicable. We stand at a fateful

juncture in the world's history, and we are at this very
moment pledging ourselves—we democratic nations in particular—to be more prudent shepherds of its future than we
have proved of its past. No better reason is needed for our
interest in that past, and in other than the doings of its kings
and ministers; since it will not be in their hands only but as
much and more in ours, strengthening them, that the fortunes
of the future, we believe, will lie.

Its nature allowed for, there is no better witness to the life
and temper of the past than drama of the time. It varies in
directness and worth. *Bartholomew Fair*, *Love for Love*, *The
Enemy of the People*, are pictures of such sections of life as the
theatre can easily accommodate. They are seen, of course,
through the eyes and coloured by the humours of Jonson and
Congreve and Ibsen; but these were not unreliable interpreters, and contemporary audiences seem to have recognized
some likeness to life. Shakespeare's Histories and Roman
plays provide, naturally, no positive evidence of how the Wars
of the Roses were actually fought or Antony betrayed and
self-betrayed; nor could the theatre in any case accommodate
more than mere symbols of such events. But they tell us what
Shakespeare, and the public he swayed, thought and felt about
these things, about kingship and empire and the passions they
nourish. And this is perhaps almost as well worth the knowing.

Students of history, no doubt, gain something indirectly by
simply *reading* the plays. But unless they are students of
drama, too, this will be of uncertain benefit; and even when
they are, of no more—to use a worn comparison—than is a
music-student's reading of a score, when he might be hearing
it performed. Nor in any case is an art something to be
cultivated for the sole benefit of its students. The language
of music and drama, and of painting and sculpture, should be
a part of the cultural currency of the educated world.

The drama's incomparable vividness—its pictures painted

in the human medium of the actors—lends to the past the actuality of the present. Further, it sets us asking: when does the past begin? By the clock, it is beginning as I speak—or as you read—these words. But of what does the past consist? Essentially, by less mechanical measurement, of the things we have done with; while what is still alive for us and within us is therefore not to be reckoned in that sort of past at all. There is a famous line in Jonson's tribute to the dead Shakespeare—'He was not for an age but for all time'—which we commonly read as conventional hyperbole (to which, incidentally, Jonson was not very prone). But it can be given a more significant meaning; and, certainly, three centuries and a half of time by the clock have told little on his value to us.

THE EXEMPLARY CASE OF SHAKESPEARE

Shakespeare did not write such plays as *Bartholomew Fair*. He preferred to set his scene in times or places where his imagination could range more freely. Yet he would give its figures familiar traits so as to 'bring them home' to us, and thus create that combination of the actual and the highly imagined in which lay his unique strength. Hamlet's Elsinore was, in particular, no far cry from the London of its staging. Bottom the Athenian weaver and Dogberry the constable of Messina might be met at the next street corner; Oswald, the sycophant upstart from about the Court of King James, is posted back intact into the England of King Lear; and Cleopatra wears a stomacher and plays billiards. These incongruities passed unremarked, since (apart from his audience's carelessness about such matters) the *life* of the characters lay, not in those circumstantial things but in the ideas and emotions informing it, which, whether or no it proves valid for 'all time', is certainly so—and has already proved so—for more than one place and age. It is astonishing how little out of touch with Shakespeare and his age we are. Upon certain questions, certainly, the Elizabethans felt as we no longer do, about kingship and its privileges, for instance; nor are we haunted, as they were, by the memory of a thirty-year civil war. If we are to appreciate the Histories we must take with us to the theatre a little historical sense—but a very little will serve. We do not think about witches quite as Macbeth did, nor about ghosts as did Hamlet. But his feelings about his mother and uncle would be ours, and his inward doubts and misgivings make a pattern (as we said) for many a man's to-day. Nor does it take modern costume to make the politics of Coriolanus modern enough.

What are the qualities in Shakespeare's plays that do most to keep them alive to-day ? He was no faultless artist nor great philosopher, nor, by direct means, a moral teacher; and devout attempts to fasten these titles on him fail. But he was a most remarkable observer; his mind, like a sensitive plate, faithfully registering every impression it received. And he was a poet—which meant among other things that his eyes saw what commoner eyes could not see, beauties they missed; and saw, beneath the surface, into men's more occult thoughts and motives. He lived and wrote at a time, too, when there was unusually much of this sort to be divined. For it was one of England's most revolutionary and formative ages, when the full effect of the belated impact of the Renaissance was first felt there, and men, in a freshly kindled awareness, were trying to come to a freer understanding of the world and themselves. Since then we may seem to have changed in so much. We have—in the clothes we wear and the way we live. The external world has changed. Air travel and radio now have their part in its organizing. England is no longer a mere little island but the hub of a great commonwealth, and the vast *terra incognita* somewhere to the west of those 'still vext Bermoothes' has become 'these United States'. We have changed in the things we *do*: but how little yet have those things changed us in what we *are*, in our ways of thinking, our moral standards, the religions we profess, our weekday creeds besides. And these are the things with which—comically coloured, tragically intensified—Shakespeare's genius dealt. We are much the same men. Caius Marcius and Menenius and the Tribunes are in politics still; and Hotspur (if without his blank verse) and Fluellen and Pistol are to be found on every battlefield. Yet change may be upon us, more of a change than lies in dress and travel and talk. A clever invention or so will not effect it, but men's views of the world and of themselves do change.[1] Medieval man—to call him so; say the man of the Crusades—gave way in time to Renaissance man. It is to his kingdom that we ourselves have belonged; and this may now in turn be giving way to another, built upon six or seven generations of an ever-encroaching industrial, mechanical, scientific civilization, culminating in two world wars. What the *spiritual* product of this will be— what type of man will emerge from its marvellous confusions —we do not yet know. Despite history's warnings he may be for complete revolution, and may relegate very much more than Shakespeare and his code to the things of the past that he has definitely done with. And in times of catastrophe changes come rapidly; so not a few of us now living may live to see the beginnings, at any rate, of such a change.

ENDURING ART

There are those of us, however, who cling to our heritage meanwhile (that being all we have), believing in the continuity of man's long progress, no matter the stumbling, up from the beast, in to-day's debt, therefore, to yesterday, and in the value to the present of that still living past. Art of all sorts has

---

[1] This was written before the disclosure of the atomic bomb.

a dominant share in keeping that past alive, in making it a part of the present. Think. A tune is played centuries ago, a sequence of notes breathed into the air, no more than that; or a poet writes a verse. Melody and verse are still alive to-day, and men are moved by them. Drama, as we said, is generously privileged in this. And if it can vivify the past—which is not past—for dwellers in the present, it can equally preserve the present for the future. The good play of to-day will have its vital value for a to-morrow, not too far in the future, also.

With this, then, we clinch the claims of a true theatre to a worthy place in the world. It can, as no other art can, help to keep us vividly conscious of the continuity of our civilization. And without this continuity, without, what is more, the consciousness of it, is it too much to say that no civilization can survive? The theatre also serves its purpose the better, when it can be made to serve it at all, even because all parties concerned must collaborate in the work. The dramatist does his share once and for all. The actor's contribution is continually renewable, and should, to his audience, seem ever to be freshly made. This presents him with a problem in the practice of his art—he only shares it, however, with all interpreters: how to combine mastery of his material with apparent spontaneity in the use of it. The problem may be insoluble in its entirety. It would occur in such a theatre as we have been envisaging, for it belongs to the finer aspects of the art. I do not attempt to deal with it, and I have refrained from speaking, except incidentally, about the art of acting at all. Frankly, the subject is too exasperating. Historical events have assembled here in America, and you are here assimilating the finest material for the making of actors, in variety of race and temperament at least, that can yet have been seen. And what is the opportunity offered to your would-be actor for his art's development? The nightly repeating, if he is lucky, of a few effective tricks of self-display, which he will attach to one character after another; and the fewer the characters he is called on to interpret the luckier a career (financially, at any rate) his will be. If that sounds too sweeping a condemnation, allow me a last comparison with the musician and his music. An actress will cheerfully walk on the stage to play Rosalind or Cleopatra with not one-tenth of the equipment in mere skill that a pianist must acquire before venturing in public upon the simplest sonata or concerto. Again: keep a master of the violin playing puerile stuff and nothing else year after year, and how long will his mastery endure? Yet again: Tchaikovsky is a most attractive composer in his way, so are Offenbach and Sullivan in theirs. But perform at concert after concert nothing except their work—or, worse, imitations of it—and where, very soon, will your musical public be? Where, moreover, would musical criticism be, and, after a while, where the musicians themselves? Doubtless the century-old round of 'classic' plays and parts, in which every aspiring actor once had to prove his quality, came to be wearisome, to audience and critics and even to the actors themselves. But in the acting of Hamlet or Benedick there was a standard of ability, to be reached or surpassed, even as there is now for the playing of the 'Emperor' concerto. And within that accustomed round the audience themselves became qualified as critics, and the actor's art as a thing in itself had some meaning for them. For acting is not to be judged merely by the momentary emotional effect it may happen to make upon the less sophisticated among us; and critical enjoyment of it is the keener kind by far.

The part to be played by a critical audience is a passive but important one. Its obligations are simple: to go to the theatre otherwise disposed, now and then, than for mere digestive entertainment and no more; to learn to like things which are good of their sort, whatever the sort, and to submit to no others. Some small amount of learning is involved; but the essentials of it can be slipped almost unnoticed into the regular course of our education, if appreciation of the arts in general is admitted once more to be a part of this. From which standpoint it is that I have been trying to discuss the use of the drama, a use depending from first to last upon our treatment of it as a normal, sane, and ordinary activity, into which may sometimes be breathed extraordinary life and beauty and spiritual power.

Postscript

I have done. You may, it strikes me, find something incongruous in a discussion of art at a time when this most destructive of wars is still raging. You cannot, believe me, find it more incongruous than I do. But artists and men of letters must resign themselves under such conditions either to going ahead with their own work and admitting its momentary uselessness or to finding other sorts of work altogether —which they will probably do worse than the next man. The personal aspect of the matter is, of course, not important, except to the one person. But to be of no present use and to have to remember that the past is of no real interest—for all their polite protests—to younger people who have never known it, is to find oneself driven forward upon the future, even though one's juniors may then reasonably retort: 'But as *you* will never know that, what concern is it of yours?' I pray their forbearance. These speculations are all they leave us to play with. It is possible, too, that our experience—which is the name we give to the record of our mistakes—may be of some indirect use to them, as a shadowy bridge between our past and their future. We elders look, according to our natures and moods, sometimes a little wistfully, sometimes, for their sakes, a little ruefully, towards that future.

THE COMING PEACE

I have never doubted that we should win this war, though God knows I had no right to take for granted the devotion of the fighting men who are winning it. Even had we British been left to fight it out alone I should still have foreseen, at the worst in some far future, and some remote mountain, another Cave of Covadonga, where a band of Christian knights would gather for such another eight hundred years' struggle as once expelled the Moslem from Spain. The world does not go backwards in its tracks; upon that at least my faith is firm. Our fight has been a fight for the future of Christian civilization, and it was bound to be won. Which of us could dare doubt it? But what of the peace? We are devising, to enable us to keep it, better machinery than ever before. That is needed, certainly; but of itself it will effect nothing. Its utility depends on the worth of the men who are to work it, upon *our* worth, and, if we mean to continue in our democratic way of life, upon the worth and wisdom of every single one of us; for that is democracy's ultimate implication. Well, not only apparently do we mean to, but we mean to shepherd other nations also into this way of life, or help restore them to it when they have lapsed from grace. And we speak sometimes of 're-educating' them. There is a certain complacency in that notion which should prompt us to a little self-questioning. Is our own education so sound, our civilization so complete, that we can be content to impose them, as they still are, upon other peoples? Certainly we have high ideals, and, in providing for the world's peace, the very best intentions. But these can make hell's pavement, as we know. On the other hand, it is idle for the sceptical critic to recommend us to perfect our own ways before we set about correcting other people's. The world will not stand still for that. But we can give more urgent thought than we have ever given yet to our shortcomings in this kind; and perhaps, with this crucial task upon us, we had better do so—while there is still time. The victors in a war are not as a rule very apt at self-examination. For ten years after the last war I lived in France, a country I love much. The French custom was to speak of November 11, not as Armistice day, the day, as we then thought it was, of deliverance, but as *le jour de la victoire*. There was nemesis in the very words. Victory this time is to lay on us an even greater responsibility than that we shouldered and let slip twenty-five years ago. Shall we be equal to it? There is a grim question.

DEMOCRACY IN THE MAKING

If we cannot make something finer of our democratic society than we have already made of it, the answer may be bluntly and bloodily: No. Democracy, as it is to-day, can hardly be called the last word in civilization. We shall be wiser to think of ours as a democracy in the making still. It has given us the forms of freedom, but these do not of themselves make us free. We are at present meshed in the machinery of many still marvellous inventions; but these, we see only too clearly, cannot of themselves civilize us, and they may but empower us to be the greater brutes. The use of freedom must be learnt, and civilization is nowhere if not within us. It is a question then, in the first place, of learning how to live, of education at its fullest. Wherever we turn for a solution of our problems, political, industrial, or social, we find ourselves—do we not?—returning to this question of education. The importance of it to the modern world was soon seen, and the dangers that lay in an uneducated democracy. During the past few hundred years we have done something to modify them. But the dangers that lie in a *half*-educated democracy, which may fancy itself educated, are perhaps greater still. And the problems of the world's immediate future centre here, since, if force is not to control it, intellect must; intellect and that less definable thing which we call 'character'. Unanimously we demand education. We are less agreed upon an answer to the question: what education is. A snowball of a notion has been set rolling—has rolled up already to a monstrous size and is hard to stop—that it consists in the accumulating of information about a lot of things we do not understand. Have we to learn what education *is* by dint of learning what it is *not*? As to the cultivating of character, that, of course, takes generations, the individual, meanwhile, acquiring a little humility, and some respect for the past.

My business with you—and thank you for your patience —has been to discuss the use of the arts in education, and of one in particular, the art of the drama. You will have gathered that I do not see much use in encouraging the average adolescent student of the humanities to give time and energy to the actual practice of the arts, painting, sculpture, music, or the drama. No harm need result, some good may; but any genuine vocation will almost certainly make itself heard without needing encouragement. And when we consider what sort of man or woman we want our education to produce—for all lies there—it will quite certainly not be the disappointed æsthete. We want, I suppose, to have the natures of the citizens of our new world cultivated to be—each one— suitably articulate, keenly critical, fully appreciative. And if we are to remain, in any true sense, individualists, it is the quality of the individual that will matter most. If democracies are to guide the world, they must represent and be represented, not so much by the 'common man', but by uncommon men—the common man made uncommon. The more of these the better. Keep the standard high; there will never be too many to wave it. The arts help us here; and our question in these lectures has been, how best to bring the influence of one among them to bear upon education, with due regard to its practical use in this but to its own lively dignity also, and without prejudice to what it can come more inspiringly to mean to a man, for the rest of his life. That is the problem in harnessing Pegasus. Art is not mere entertainment, although it can be most entertaining. It is a moral exercise, although it need never be depressingly solemn. It should leaven the daily life of a community. It frees men's imagination, and controls it. If it is of good quality itself it sets a standard of quality, even in the simplest things. 'Quality' is its watchword. There will be the difference between a nature it influences and one to which it means nothing that is the difference between crude iron and tempered steel.